THE EARLY YEARS
Laying the foundations for racial equality

Iram Siraj-Blatchford

Trentham Books

Trentham Books Limited

Westview House	22883 Quicksilver Drive
734 London Road	Sterling
Oakhill	VA 20166-2012
Stoke on Trent	USA
Staffordshire	
England ST4 5NP	

First published 1994, reprinted 1995, 1999, 2002, 2003 and 2005

British Library Cataloguing-in-Publication Data
A catalogue record for this book is available from the British Library

0 948080 64 7

Designed and typeset by Trentham Print Design Ltd., Chester and printed in Great Britain by Cromwell Press Ltd., Wiltshire.

To
the Children of Bosnia
and
my mother
my first and best teacher

Contents

Foreword by *Gillian Pugh*   xi
Preface   xiii
Acknowledgements   xv

SECTION I — UNDERSTANDING RACISM

Chapter 1 Young Children and Racial Difference   3
   Children's attitudes to racial difference   4
   Children, self-identity and self-esteem   6
   Young children's experience of racism   9

Chapter 2 Understanding Racial Inequality   13
   The Power of History   13
   Different and Unequal   16
   Normalising racism   22
   Mass Media   23
   Language   26
   Jokes and graffiti   28
   Art and literature   28

SECTION II — TOWARDS GOOD PRACTICE

Chapter 3 **Language, Learning and Multilingual Development**   33

How important is language?   33
Language development and young children   34
Language Development Versus Linguistic Prejudice and Racism   42
Bilingual and Multilingual Children   45
What is this thing called bilingualism or multilingualism?   46
Monolingual educators and bilingual children —   49
a contradiction in terms?
Creating a multilingual ethos   50
Staff checklist for creating multilingual support in the   51
early years

Chapter 4 **Creating a Curriculum and Ethos for Racial Equality**   61

What is education for?   61
Child-centredness   64
Planning for and developing a relevant curriculum   67
The importance of concrete experience and play   73
Social interaction and small group work   74
Stories, books and language awareness   76
Posters, puzzles and toys   80
The 'homecorner'   80
Festivals   82
Snack times and cooking   82
Music, rhymes and songs   84
Values and behaviour   85
Child profiles and assessment   88

Chapter 5 **Parental Involvement: Fostering Confidence and**   91
Communication

Parents' preconceived views on education   93
Power, participation and access   95
The changing needs of families   98
Helping parents to deal with their own racism   100
Supporting black and ethnic minority parents   102
Cultural diversity and childrearing   102
Ethnic minority parents as educators to staff   105
Parents and their home language   106

SECTION III: POLICIES, LEGISLATION AND TRAINING

Chapter 6 **Antiracism: Policy Developments in The Early Years**   109
    Why is policy important?   110
    National Children's Bureau Early Childhood Unit   112
    National Nursery Examination Board (NNEB)   116
    Pre-school Playgroups Association (PPA)   121
    National Childminding Association (NCMA)   124
    What have we learnt?   126

Chapter 7 **The State in Three Acts**
    Institutional 'race' and gender bias in child care and education   130
    services
    The Race Relations Act (1976)   131
    The Children Act (1989)   133
    Racial Equality and the Children Act   135
    Implementing the Children Act to promote equality   136
    Education Reform Act (1988) (ERA)   139
    What is the purpose of the ERA?   140
    The National Curriculum   141
    School assessments and black and ethnic minority children   144
    Teacher education and training   145
    Local Management of Schools (LMS)   146
    The Parents' Charter   146
    The role of Governors   148

Chapter 8 **Training and Resources: The Way Forward**   149
    The 'E' in Equality   149
    Ourselves — a good starting point   150
    Training activities for educators   154
    The process by which change occurs — an example   163
    Working together for change   163

Useful Sources and Resources for Racial Equality   167
Bibliography   171
Index   179

Foreword

How we feel about ourselves as individuals — our sense of identity and our self-esteem — is closely bound up with how others see us and the feedback that they give us. This developing sense of self-worth is one of the most important aspects — perhaps the most important aspect — of growing up between birth and the age of seven or eight. Children begin to form attitudes towards themselves and others from what they see and hear around them — from their families and their friends, from books and the media. For many children this learning includes racial attitudes, and we now know that many children as young as three or four are beginning to feel discriminated against. The racism that is inherent, often in hidden ways, in all aspects of society is making young children understand that there are differences between black and white, and that black children are less highly valued than white children.

Racism affects black children — but it also affects white children, who may be growing up with a false sense of their own superiority and acquiring views based on unacceptable stereotypes if they are not shown alternative ways of thinking and behaving. We cannot say in predominantly white areas that 'it's not an issue here', for we all live in a multicultural society and racism is an issue for us all.

This is an important and accessible book which provides thoughtful and practical support for early years workers. The Children Act provides the legal framework for developing policies which value and respect each child's racial origin, religion, culture and language, and the Race Relations

Act supports us in challenging discrimination. But for many who work with children, whether in schools, day nurseries, playgroups or as child-minders, the legal framework is not enough. Educators need to know not only that racism affects all children, and that the early years are the best time to confront it — but also how to ensure equality of opportunity for all children. This is the question that we in the Early Childhood Unit at the National Children's Bureau get asked above all others, and this is the question that this book seeks to answer.

In identifying the many ways in which young children experience racism, in looking at good practice in language development, curriculum development and working with parents, in identifying the importance of policies that really are implemented, and the importance of training and resources to take these policies forward, this book provides the key building blocks for 'laying the foundations for racial equality'.

Gillian Pugh
Director, Early Childhood Unit, National Children's Bureau.

Preface

This book is written for a multi-professional audience. Over the last ten years I have found myself providing lectures and workshops on anti-racism, multilingual education and care to a variety of groups around the country. In all these interactions with teachers, headteachers, child-minders, nursery nurses, playgroup leaders, social workers, policy makers and trainers, similar and recurring themes have emerged. My audiences and workshop participants have invariably been interested in issues of curriculum, policy development, parental involvement and training. This book attempts to respond fully to the questions that were asked and to offer practical guidance on practice.

Although the text is primarily aimed at practitioners, trainers and policy makers, it has been informed by and refers to relevant research and theory. This knowledge is intended to provide concrete foundations for our ongoing development of practice. Most academics in the UK who have written about 'race' and education have so far neglected the early years and yet it is here that some of the most exciting work and change is taking place.

My title reflects my most important reason for writing this book: I believe that by 'laying the foundations' for racial equality in the early years we are making a major investment for future racial harmony and for the development of a confident and well-informed citizenship. We tend to think only of bigger people as citizens or those worthy of teaching important concepts such as justice and equality, yet it is during the early years that the foundations for these attitudes are laid.

Throughout this book the term 'educator' refers to all who educate and care for young children. The category therefore includes parents, nursery nurses, childminders and playgroup leaders as well as teachers. This multidisciplinary/multi professional approach is also reflected in the adoption of the term 'setting' which is used to signify the diverse locations within which children learn. Typical 'settings' therefore include the home, day care centres, nurseries and schools.

Section I and II of the book are informative and intended to build confidence and understanding of what racism is and how to deal with it positively through our everyday practice with children. Section III is more concerned with understanding the national initiatives which support or hinder equality. The final chapter on training is also practical and should be read in conjunction with Sections I and II.

I have tried to incorporate the ideas and views of academics and practitioners from overseas, chiefly from the United States and Australia, as well as the findings of research studies carried out in the UK. Most of all I have relied on my own experience of working with children in nurseries and primary schools and with practitioners, trainers and policy makers in developing good practice. Practice which does not undermine any child because of racism.

Iram Siraj-Blatchford

Acknowledgements

This book would not have been possible without the support of a great number of people. I am grateful to the key organisations and the colleagues within them that I have worked with and learnt from. The National Children's Bureau, National Nursery Examinations Board (now the Council for Awards in Childcare and Education); Pre-school Playgroups Association and the National Childminding Association deserve special mention. I am particularly grateful to the children, parents and staff at Hillfields Nursery Centre in Coventry whose support and generous contribution, in allowing me to photograph and constantly learn from their work, has greatly benefited this book. My greatest thanks go to my family (I have several weekends to make up to them!), to Gillian Klein my editor for her patience, support and good humour and finally to John Siraj-Blatchford for his love, occasional secretarial and moral support and for valuable comments on drafts, for providing me with hot meals, gallons of hot tea and for sometimes even doing my share of the housework.

SECTION I
Understanding Racism

CHAPTER 1

Young Children and Racial Difference

Six three year olds sat around a table in a large nursery school in a shire county playing with playdough. A mother helper sat with them talking to individual children about their 'work', explaining, encouraging and taking joy in the children's learning and talk. Jennifer was going to be four years old the following week. She began to enthuse about her forthcoming birthday party. Mark, Sarah, Kylie and Nathan were going to be sent invitations to attend her special day. Nisha, a child of South Asian parentage was not mentioned. Kylie reminded Jennifer that Nisha had not been invited. Looking at Nisha, Jennifer said, 'My mummy doesn't want any blackies in the house.' After a momentary silence, the parent helper, looking nervous and agitated, responded by saying: 'That's not a very nice thing to say! Nisha isn't very dark anyway.' Everyone continued with the activity as if nothing had happened, except Nisha. The look on Nisha's face was one of hurt, confusion and bewilderment. No-one had considered her feelings, supported or comforted her or explained that being black was not bad in itself. She was left to come to terms, all by herself, with the association of being 'a black' and being unacceptable — at the age of three. No attempt had been made to explain to Jennifer why what she had said was wrong.

The way children see themselves and the way others see them is crucial to their development. It is the way in which children construct an image of themselves and others and form their self-identity. They are affected by the value others put on the way they speak, dress and look. Although it is possible to change the way they do things, e.g. speak or dress, it is not possible to change how they look. They cannot change their physical characteristics. The whole concept of 'race' categorisation of people is based solely on physiological differences. That is, the colour of their skin, the type of hair they have or their facial features. These are then used to distinguish one racial group from another.

Robert Miles (1982) is one of many who have criticised the scientific development of human categorisation and particularly the social understandings and status accorded to particular 'races'. In fact it is now widely accepted by scientists that there is no genetic basis to any such categories and that 'race' is indeed only skin deep. In grouping people we accord them more or less status. White scientists invented racial categories and, given the history of the white domination and exploitation of black people, they put themselves at the top of their racial hierarchy. As we shall see, most British people still believe or act according to this racist structure. Chapter 2 deals with this issue more thoroughly.

How does this affect young children or those who work with them? The basis on which educators judge and work with children is often influenced by the way the educator and the children perceive racial difference.

Children's attitudes to racial difference

Contrary to popular belief that early childhood is a time of innocence, even the very youngest children are constantly learning from what and who is around them. They learn not only from what we intend to teach but from all of their experiences. If black people are treated differently from white people then children will absorb the difference as part of their world view. To deny this effect is to deny that children are influenced by their socialisation.

Research evidence produced by David Milner (1983), a social psychologist, and Jocelyn Maximé (1991), a clinical psychologist, shows that children have learned positive and negative feelings about racial groups from an early age. Milner (1983), suggests that children as young as three

4

demonstrate an awareness of a racial hierarchy 'in line with current adult prejudices' (p122,1983). This hierarchy places white at the top and black at the bottom. Maximé (1991) argues that some black children can be severely damaged by their view that there are people around them who do not value them because they are black.

This would suggest that early years educators need to offer all children guidance and support in developing positive attitudes towards all people, and in particular black people. A focus on similarities is as important as dealing with human difference. The early years is an appropriate time to develop this work with young children. In fact early years philosophy and experts encourage developing the whole child. Margaret Lally (1991) asserts that only highly trained people should be considered appropriate educators of the young. It is also important to recognise that all those who work with young children, trained or not, play a crucial role in educating them, because children learn in all contexts. Similarly it can be argued that all those who regard themselves as educators of the young play a vital role in caring for them. The divide between child 'care' and 'education' is a false one, and ideally anyone who works with children should be well trained.

Lally devotes a whole chapter in her book, *The Nursery Teacher in Action* (1991) to the need to develop an early years environment which supports emotional and physical security. Rightly, she claims that children cannot learn effectively without such an approach and that this means the educator must be flexible enough to cater for a wide range of needs. Audrey Curtis (1991) reminds us of the philosophy of early childhood pioneers such as Margaret MacMillan and Froebel, upon whose ideas the principles of our early years education and care are built. Again the prime importance of the whole child is stressed. The need for emotional, social, physical, moral, aesthetic and mental well-being all go hand in hand. Any early years curriculum should therefore incorporate work on children's awareness of racial difference. Child-centredness in this sense is not only inward looking but takes account also of the children's social world; it is reflexive.

The Early Years Curriculum Group (1989) highlight ten principles which guide early years educators. Three of these are particularly pertinent:

1. *The whole child is considered to be important — social, emotional, physical, intellectual and moral development are interrelated.*

2. *Learning is holistic and for the young child is not compartmentalised under subject headings.*

3. *The child's education is seen as an interaction between the child and the environment, which includes people as well as materials and knowledge.*

For these reasons dealing with racial attitudes which are negative is crucial. At the same time all early years educators should be promoting positive racial awareness for each child and between children.

Some early years educators fear that working against racism with children might be seen as working against the home because the children's racism might have come from parents. This attitude depends largely on the educators' own understanding of racism. If it is understood by educators that racism causes long term damage to children and is unacceptable conduct in our society, that it denies basic human rights and diminishes the life-chances of some people, then it follows that it must be dealt with. We have no doubt that once we know about child abuse by a parent towards their child, be it physical, emotional or sexual, intrusive action must be taken. We accept that this would be working against the parent's wishes but would not feel deterred, because abuse is against the law and contravenes children's rights to a secure environment. Similarly, racism is against the law and unacceptable. Early years educators need to define clear guidance on how to work with parents and children towards an anti-racist environment (see Diagram 1, opposite).

Children, self-identity and self-esteem

The way children feel about themselves is learned. Many writers, such as Lawrence (1987) and Burns (1982) have shown that positive self-esteem depends upon whether children feel that others accept them and see them as competent and worthwhile. Researchers have also shown the connection between academic achievement and self-esteem. Purkey (1970) correlates high self-esteem with high academic performance. Black children's poor academic performance has been well documented in the Swann

Black and ethnic minority experience of racism in society

To understand why this is an important issue we need to take account of the cycle of racism as experienced by many Black and ethnic minority groups. A cycle of this nature may include the following experiences.

Black parents are subjected to racism in jobs, housing services etc.

Black/ethnic minorities as role models in powerful positions are virtually non-existent.

The media perpetuates stereotypes through images and omission of ethnic minorities.

Structural, cultural and interpersonal racism is not dealt with. The Race Relations Act is difficult to enforce.

White people appear to be unaware of their history and take their attitudes to be normal.

Young children, both white and black absorb racist values as young as three years of age.

Racism is seen as normal through our culture: jokes, grafitti, literature eg. *Robinson Crusoe*, media — Hollywood films etc.

Report (1985) and elsewhere the link between racism and underachievement has been thoroughly argued. However, if those who work with young children are able to undermine children's self-esteem through racist behaviour then we have to evaluate our actions very carefully. Positive action to promote self-esteem should form an integral part of work with children and ought to be incorporated into everyday curriculum.

Maximé (1991) has argued that over 95% of young black children are 'British black' yet are always referred to as 'Asians' or 'Afro-Caribbeans' rather than according to their true identity. She argues that racial identity is the solid foundation upon which further learning is built. She states that:

> Whether we are a builder or not we observe that the first area of focus is in constructing a foundation. A solid foundation is comparable to one's identity, that inner core which like a foundation to a building must be properly constructed and nurtured from inception(p4 1991).

Geneva Gay (1985) has similarly argued that children's ethnic identity affects their whole development and learning and that it should be seen as a vital part of each child's development.

Some research data suggests that children's attitudes and self-identity can be affected by societal stereotyping of racial groups. Cross (1985), cited in Dermon-Sparks (1989), argues that there are two distinguishable effects of racism on black children's identity. The first is personal identity which includes self-esteem, confidence and self-evaluation and the second is reference group orientation which develops racial identity, race esteem and racial ideology. Cross analyses studies on black children's self-identity and establishes that most of the studies are about reference group orientation and not personal identity. Cross also suggests that black children's self-identity is on a par with white children's but that their reference group orientation is low and that this has a damaging effect on black children's ability to counter the impact of racism on their life experiences (p4 1989).

This is not to suggest that only black children are damaged by racism. Although only a few studies have been carried out on the effects of racism on white children, they reveal that white children too can be damaged psychologically. Kutner (1955) and other researchers have shown that young white children who are racist have a distorted perception of reality and their ability to judge and reason is also affected.

Some researchers have dismissed work carried out with black children on a non-academic curriculum related to racial identity as a waste of time. This critical writing is predominantly aimed at those who teach older children. Maureen Stone's (1981) book is typical of this writing. She asserts that a multicultural curriculum distracts from the real reasons for black children's underachievement, that is, insufficient access and teaching of academic subjects. She suggests that a 'black studies' approach to teaching has been adopted as one way of controlling disaffected children rather than teaching them.

None of these arguments apply to the under-sevens, where it is widely assumed and recognised that a more integrated, holistic and developmental approach is needed to learning, teaching and care.

Young children's experience of racism

How do young children who are in our care experience racism? This is a question that most educators ask. We know that children absorb racist knowledge and understanding from their environment. This can be from parental views, media images, and the child's own perceptions of the way black people are seen and treated. In the absence of strong and positive black role models children may be left with a rather negative perception of black people.

The most common form of racism young black children experience is through racist name-calling or through negative references by white children (or adults) to their colour, language or culture. Educators may hear some of these remarks and it is vital that these are dealt with appropriately as they arise.

Early years educators are often inexperienced and lack knowledge and understanding in dealing with these matters. They often display a profound sense of inadequacy when faced with racism from children. They may also doubt whether racist name-calling is any more damaging than any other form. While all forms and types of name-calling are wrong and should be dealt with, racist name-calling is a cause for particular concern. Educators should be informed of the research evidence which illustrates why it is a special case and what we can do about it.

After the murder of Ahmed Ullah, a thirteen year old boy who was stabbed to death by a white boy in their school playground, a number of studies have been carried out which highlight the effects and prevalence of racist name-calling and racist harassment on the daily lives of school children (Kelly, 1988; Troyna and Hatcher, 1992; Wright, 1992). It is evident from the death of Ahmed Ullah (and others) that we can not ignore the root cause of such abhorrent tragedies. In each such case there are two victims, the victim of racism and the dehumanised racist as a victim of a racist society. As Troyna and Hatcher, in Gill, et al (1992) point out:

> The murder of black youngsters by white students in Britain is a rare occurrence. Racist harassment is not, however. It is common: a pervasive, even everyday, experience of many students of Afro-Caribbean and South Asian origin in and around schools in this country (p188,1992).

This is not a phenomenon experienced only by older children; it is just that most research has been conducted with older primary and secondary children. However, recent research has focused on the under-sevens. Cecile Wright's (1992) research looked at the experience of black children in nursery and primary schools. She selected four schools, three taking three to eight year olds and one middle school. Wright observed a total of 970 children and 57 staff and conducted interviews with a selection of staff and children.

Wright offers a detailed analysis of her study. Her findings are disturbing because she has produced clear evidence that it is not only children who behave in a racist manner but also some of their teachers. She concludes that both African-Caribbean and South Asian children experience racism. In particular she found that teachers criticised African-Caribbean children (especially the boys) more than other children. Teachers also held negative stereotypes of South Asian children as lacking in cognitive ability and having poor linguistic and social skills. In terms of relations with other children she found that:

> Racist name-calling and attacks from white peers were a regular, almost daily, experience for Asian children. Teachers were aware of the racial harassment experienced by Asian pupils, but were reluctant to formally address this issue. (p40, 1992).

It is hardly surprising that Wright concludes:

> It is generally accepted that the foundations of emotional, intellectual and social development are laid in the early years of formal education.

The kind of education a child receives at this stage, therefore, is considered to be of greatest importance. From the evidence gathered in connection with this project, it could be argued that some black children are relatively disadvantaged at this stage of their education (p40,1992).

In a study on playground behaviour, Ross and Ryan (1990) highlight very similar findings about racist name-calling and stereotyping during play-time: children had absorbed stereotypes of South Asian girls as passive and quiet and of African- Caribbean boys as aggressive.

Unfortunately there is no reason to assume that children who are in early years settings other than nurseries and schools are not having similar experiences. In my own experience as a nursery and infant teacher and now as a teacher educator I have seen, and still hear from my students, the effects of racism on young children's lives. Students, teachers, child-minders and playgroup workers have often asked how they can deal with racial harassment. The first step is to recognise that the problem exists. Davey (1983) states quite clearly that a system of racial categorisation and classification exists which acts as an irresistible tool by which children can simplify and make meaning of their social world, unless educators can offer a carefully planned and co-ordinated approach to promote an anti-racist perspective throughout their work.

It would be a great mistake to assume that this is only a 'problem' in largely multi-ethnic settings. Recent research by Barry Troyna and Richard Hatcher (1992), *Racism in Children's Lives* is a study of mainly white primary schools. They illustrate through their study that although racism is prevalent in the lives of children, children also have a strong egalitarian sense on which educators can build through anti-racist strategies. They argue that clear and strong policies for dealing with racist behaviour are necessary, as well as curriculum strategies which allow all children to discuss, understand and deal with oppressive behaviour aimed at particular groups such as: black children, girls, the disabled and younger children. Cohn (1988) also suggests that educators should make opportunities for stressing similarities as well as differences.

Part 2 of this book discusses how to deal with racist incidents, how to create an anti-racist curriculum and gives attention to the involvement of parents.

CHAPTER 2

Understanding Racial Inequality

In order to understand why racism exists today, and how we can begin to counter its damaging effects, we need to look at our past. A past in which racist ideology was normalised to justify the exploitation of some groups for the material gains of others. We also need to understand how the prejudice and misinformation continues today and how this is passed on to younger generations. Only then can we begin to set the record straight, understand our own views and begin working effectively in laying the foundations for a more just beginning for our young children.

The Power of History

The term 'race' first came to be used in English in the 16th century. During this time massive social and cultural changes were taking place in Europe. Relations between the western and non-western worlds were being transformed, as newly discovered lands and populations became increasingly dominated and exploited (Rattansi 1992). How did this happen, and what was the motivating factor for Britain and other Europeans? The answer lies largely in the greed of Europeans to make wealth for themselves. In the process they stigmatised certain 'race' groups as inferior and sub-human, so as to justify their exploitation. The term 'race' acquired a pseudo-scientific status as part of an elaborate and more or less systematic doctrine of human classification.

For Europe's white explorers, to 'discover' new lands meant to possess them. They claimed that the lands and peoples had been provided 'by the grace of God', entirely for their purposes. They did not acknowledge the rights of the people who already lived in these lands. Europeans assumed they could do with the land, its wealth and its people precisely as they wished. Early years practitioners will no doubt recognise this morally under-developed attitude of 'finders keepers'. The slave trade which followed the 'discovery' of Africa inflicted dreadful brutality and degradation on the black population. It has been estimated that a total of ten million people were transported in this trade and that millions were killed during transportation in cramped and dehumanising conditions aboard ships set for America and the Caribbean. The ruthless colonisation of the Americas demanded a supply of labour for the labour intensive crops of cotton and sugar and for mining. As millions of black people slaved in the homes of whites and on their plantations, the wealth created by the products exported helped to fuel the industrial growth of Europe. It is sad and ironic that today some of our politicians still criticise people from the exploited areas of the world for wanting to make a life in Britain. In the face of the atrocities faced by native Americans in America and Canada, the Aborigines in Australia and black South Africans in their own countries, it is evident that the British have rarely seen the world from a black person's perspective.

We read these accounts today and see the gross inhumanity perpetrated. But in the 18th and 19th centuries biologists and scientists were busily justifying their actions by describing black people as sub-human and associating blackness with shame, ugliness, bestiality and sinister deeds (Crispin, 1986). It is ironic that on many occasions when I have asked young black children how they felt at being called a racist name they have said 'I felt ashamed' or 'I felt sad'. Perpetrators of racist name-calling are using the power of history to hurt, because to date we have done so little to set the record straight, to bring up our children with a proper understanding of their historical heritage.

By the 19th century Britain had a huge Empire which incorporated much of South East Asia, Africa and the Caribbean. All the black peoples of the Empire continued to be regarded as inferior, and as subjects of the Empire whose only purpose of existence was assumed to be to serve the Empire. As Sally Tomlinson (1990) has argued, at this same time beliefs in biological and intellectual superiority were accompanied by beliefs in cultural superiority. Tomlinson cites the views and influence of Lord MacCauley, who in 1833 stated that the British Empire illustrated the *'triumph of reason over barbarianism'*. He wanted to see the Empire promoting as superior the arts, morals, law and literature of Britain. By 1835 MacCauley had ensured that education in India would be based on Western literature and scientific knowledge, and taught in the English language. The ordinary British people were made to feel superior; they were told by their teachers that they were the best, the most intelligent, the most civilised and the most advanced. Schools celebrated 'Empire Day' each year (in some areas as recently as the 1940s), a day of celebrations when outside speakers came in to tell children about the 'civilising' effects of the Empire upon the colonies.

Even with the demise of the British Empire the legacy of white superiority lives on. Britain may have let go of some of her lands in name but there is still a strong influence through the educational, legal and trade systems established. In Britain today some of our members of parliament still reveal their racist view of black British people. As Paul Gilroy (1987) points out, ideas of 'the enemy within', 'the unarmed invasion', 'alien encampments', 'swamping', 'alien territory' and 'new commonwealth occupation' have all been used to describe the black presence. Enoch Powell, Norman Tebbit and Margaret Thatcher's contributions have been typical but far from exceptional.

In 1978 Mrs Thatcher assumed that she was talking for the (white) British people when she said:

People are really rather afraid that this country might be rather swamped by people with a different culture. The British culture has done so much for democracy, for law and so much throughout the world that if there is any fear that it might be swamped people are going to be rather hostile to those coming in. So if you want good race relations you have got to allay people's fears on numbers.

15

Consider this view in the light of Britain's colonial history and it is clear that some still wish to hold on to false notions of superiority. They have learned nothing from the past.

Since 1976 we have had a Race Relations Act in Britain but the government itself is exempt from its provisions and since 1962 immigration acts have progressively curbed the rights of black people and other ethnic minority groups. Most black people in this country are British born, and over 95% of black under-sevens were born here. It is high time that we recognised that black people are British. Those who came originally from the colonies were invited by the British Government after the Second World War because Britain needed cheap labour once more. So it is not in the least surprising that black people and some white people want to do something about racism and the false foundations upon which it has been built.

Different and Unequal

We have seen how prejudice and stereotyping developed historically and how they worked against black people. The implications for society today are still far-reaching and affect the life chances and material conditions for black citizens in Britain. We can see this if we look at the disadvantages suffered by black people through discrimination in such sectors of public life as employment, housing, health, care and education.

Institutional racism is not the sort of racism that is overt, such as name-calling or violent acts against black people. It is much more subtle and very pervasive. It could be defined as the policies and everyday practices of institutions — such as early childhood organisations, nurseries or universities — that work to perpetuate racial inequality without actually acknowledging that unfair practices are taking place, or that unfair procedures exist. However, the recognition that institutional racism exists has prompted many institutions, including those responsible for early childhood education and care, to devise racial equality policies.

It is beyond the scope of this chapter to look at all of the vast amount of research evidence that has been collated over the last thirty years about institutional racism in every sector of public life. Nevertheless, it is worth surveying some evidence of the consequences of institutional racism on the lives of black families in Britain, to illustrate the severe discrimination which exists. We will focus on employment, housing and education, all of which contribute to the quality of life we experience.

Most of Britain's black population still live in the large industrial cities to which they were invited to take up menial employment positions in the 1950s. But employment patterns have changed considerably since the 1950s and Britain has been through recurring periods of high unemployment. When unemployment rises, the number of black people out of work increases more rapidly than among the rest of the population. In 1983 the Home Office Report, *Ethnic Minorities in Britain* highlighted the discrimination experienced by black people in the job market. It not only indicated higher levels of unemployment amongst African-Caribbean and South Asian people but showed that they were also likely to receive lower salaries than their white counterparts. The report showed that black people are more likely to have to work longer hours and do more shifts to make the same money as whites and are in posts which are, on average, less secure and concentrated in older industries.

Another report published in 1984 by the Policy Studies Institute (PSI) presents a similarly depressing picture of the economic position of black people. The report shows that the opportunities for black people's employment have hardly changed at all since the 1950s. They are still concentrated in the worst jobs and experience twice the rate of unemployment that white people do. As a result black people suffer from poverty disproportionately, and their chances of moving to look for other jobs are therefore poor too. Of course this is not true for all black people, but success is still a possibility for only the minority. McIntosh and Smith (1974) showed that South Asians and African-Caribbeans faced discrimination in 46% of cases when applying for unskilled job vacancies, demonstrating quite clearly the level of racial discrimination in the area of employment.

Inequality in employment is not only suffered by black unskilled workers. A more recent report by the Commission for Racial Equality (CRE) by Brennan and McGeevor (1987) about the employment of graduates from different ethnic minority groups, in their first year, reveals that black graduates found it more difficult to get a job than graduates who were white. Black graduates who did secure employment often did so at lower levels than their qualification fitted them for and at lower salaries. From this evidence it could be argued that discrimination in employment is widespread. The CRE has urged employers to scrutinise their practices e.g. of admission, selection, interviewing and promotion, in an effort to stop discriminatory procedures working in favour of white candidates, and to ensure equality of opportunity for all.

The CRE have investigated discrimination in employment, housing and education and any member of the public can have access to the dozens of reports they have produced in these areas, as well as others such as the health service. Housing for black people is another area of major disadvantage. Many will have heard about or remember the racism faced by some black people when they first arrived in Britain, the 'No Blacks' signs alongside some advertisements for rooms or flats (Carter 1986). Since the 1976 Race Relations Act now forbids discrimination on the basis of colour we might be mistakenly led into thinking that these things only occurred in the past.

It is true that people can no longer put up signs that say 'No Blacks', and no longer do we find it acceptable, at least not publicly, for politicians to use slogans which present housing black people as something hateful and undesirable, as Peter Griffiths did during the 1964 General Election in his Smethwick constituency. Griffiths secured his seat on a campaign which included the slogan 'If you want a nigger neighbour vote Labour' (Cashmore & Troyna, 1990). Yet there is more recent evidence that racism is still widely prevalent in housing.

The two reports cited earlier, *Ethnic Minorities in Britain* (1983) and *Black and White Britain* (1984) provide clear evidence that the original relegation of South Asian and African-Caribbean Britons to particular jobs and residential areas continues to generate among the population certain expectations and behaviour which perpetuate inequality. The 1983 report found evidence that black people were still often charged more by landlords/ladies for inferior accommodation, that discrimination in the private sector and council housing is still common and that generally black people occupy some of the poorest, overcrowded and run-down homes. News reports often alert us to the disproportionate number of homeless, and those facing racial harassment among the black communities of Britain.

In surveying the evidence on employment and housing, some readers may be tempted to assert that some of the evidence cited applies also to conditions in which some white people find themselves. No one could, or should, deny that white working class people suffer discrimination too. But there is no doubt that black people are over-represented in the poorer classes and face the additional discrimination of racism as well as class prejudice, and that they can encounter racism whatever their class background.

The debate around inequality in education has focused on evidence of the underachievement of particular racial groups in our education system. Cashmore and Troyna (1990) define educational underachievement as:

> The level a student reaches as measured by scores on various tests and examinations. Black (African-Caribbean) children in the UK are known for their persistent underachievement for they tend as a group to score less in examinations relative to white and South Asian pupils (p125,1990).

The Report of the Committee of Inquiry into the Education of Children from Ethnic Minority Groups, known as *The Swann Report* (1985), compiled evidence from the School Leavers Survey Exercise 1978/9 from six local education authorities in inner London comprising half the ethnic minority school leavers. The findings confirmed that African-Caribbean children as a group were performing consistently worse than South Asians and whites.

According to the statistics only 3% of African-Caribbean school leavers in 1978/9 were achieving the GCSE equivalent ('O' level) higher grade passes compared to 18% of South Asian and 16% of all other groups. There was a very similar pattern for 'A' level results, where African-Caribbeans left school with only 2% having pass grades, compared to an average of 13% South Asian and 12% of all other groups. Sally Tomlinson (1980) in a review on the studies on ethnic minority educational achievement, pointed out that 26 out of 33 studies on the performance of African-Caribbean children in our education system show that they perform less well in tests and examinations and that they are under-represented in the higher streams of schools and over-represented in 'education for special needs' schools.

There have been many problems associated with the interpretation of these studies. Firstly, the statistics are based on culturally biased tests which include end of school examinations. This has been an enduring problem in education and here is not the place for a lengthy discussion about it. However, the Swann Report (1985) recommends that exam boards should review their policies with respect to making their syllabuses and examination papers more relevant to the actual experiences of the children in our schools today, so as to minimise the effects of cultural bias in school tests. Many African-Caribbeans who gave evidence to the Committee of the Swann Inquiry also cited racism as a major reason for their children's underachievement. The report recognised that teacher racism, low expectations and the stereotyping of black children could have important bearings on children's school performance.

According to Reeves and Chevannes (1981) another difficulty in interpreting the statistics has been the anxiety of some researchers to illustrate educational difference on the grounds of race, without incorporating the influence that social class background can have. This may go some way toward explaining why some South Asian groups, such as Bangladeshi children, continue to underachieve but, equally, other researchers have tried to show how, even when class is taken into account, black children disproportionately underachieve in comparison to similar class groups of white children (Craft & Craft 1981). It is clear from the evidence in the Swann Report, that African-Caribbean and Bangladeshi children underachieve in education.

The Swann Report (1985) also reveals the perceptions of some African-Caribbean students (already in higher education) about the reasons underlying 'success' or 'failure' in schools. Students felt that their experiences in school disadvantaged them. They questioned the system; as one student put it: '...*I was the only one.. in an A stream in my year and the majority of black children were in the bottom stream...but why was it that all these black children were in lower classes, there must be something wrong...*' Able black youngsters sometimes doubted their own ability because of the way black children are stereotyped. One student recalled some of these tensions:

> I also think it affects the children's self-image...I am a classic example because I was put in a low stream when I started school and when I came first in class I was quite amazed because I thought the teacher was doing me a favour because he liked me. And when it happened on numerous occasions and I eventually reached the top stream, all the time I kept thinking I should be in the bottom stream because I still haven't got the capability because all the black kids up to then

were all in the lower stream. Like on prize-giving I still never got in coming first (in class) any kind of recognition in terms of prize, but I got prizes for sport and dance.

Asked why South Asian children were not always associated with low streams in secondary education, one student replied:

> It is expectation again because Asians have always been recognised as having a valid civilisation whereas people from the Caribbean have not, so it is a racial expectation which is different.

These examples are a sad reflection of the way some teachers stereotype African-Caribbeans as being good at 'physical' activities such as sport but not at academic work. Another student tried to explain why, if one black child can succeed academically, teachers still do not expect most of them to:

> People like us who make it through the system... the teachers will say.. 'But you are different'. Instead of changing their attitudes about black people they make an exception of you...They don't make an assessment that...perhaps we might be a bit wrong about this (Swann Report, 1985).

As these students suggest, racial inequality in education is more complicated than statistics can reveal. The CRE continues to identify institutional racism and discriminatory practices at all levels of education and not just in school examinations. Let us look at just three cases of proven discriminatory practice.

☐ In 1986 the CRE completed a formal investigation into Calderdale LEA. The CRE found that Calderdale's separate arrangements for teaching children English as a second language (ESL) in their schools were unlawful under the Race Relations Act (1976). Educating children outside the mainstream of school education denied them the right to a broad and balanced curriculum. The CRE also pointed out that children learn a second language more readily if they are supported in the mainstream of education along with their peers, using the most natural models of language. The Secretary of State for Education accepted this finding and Calderdale now has integrated its ESL work into the mainstream. Unfortunately there are still many LEAs that carry on the discriminatory practice of segregated ESL provision, and the CRE does not have the funds or the personnel to take on all such cases.

☐ Another example of discrimination in education was taken up after some black parents complained to the CRE that the procedures for admission to secondary schools in the south west division of Hertfordshire LEA were unfair. Two grant-maintained schools were found guilty of discriminating against South Asian applicants because of the schools' insistence on reasons for application being submitted in a written letter. The CRE found that because some South Asian parents had difficulty writing in English their applications were considered less favourably, because they often submitted shorter letters offering fewer reasons for their child's admission. The presence of siblings in the school was shown to be a further discriminatory factor, as many of the South Asian families had only recently settled in the area.

☐ Finally, a survey the CRE supported, of the perceptions of black students on teacher training courses, reported systematic disillusionment among black students over the racism they faced in their teacher education course and student services. The study pointed to the need for long term planning by institutions to address recruitment and selection procedures, racist attitudes among staff and students and on teaching practice (Siraj-Blatchford, 1991).

The evidence cited in this section represents only the tip of an enormous iceberg of racism. The reader may be wondering why racism continues to be perpetuated and manifested in all these and other forms, given the grossly damaging effects that it has had on the life chances of our black community. How does it happen and how do children perceive, internalise and reflect the racism prevalent in our history and present day society?

Normalising racism

We have seen how racism can work in institutions and be perpetuated in a cyclical way — often termed structural racism. It is embedded within the very fabric of our society and is largely hidden. Our understanding of racial inequality can be further enhanced if we explore more overt forms of racism. In chapter 1 we looked at racist name-calling and the effects this has on children's lives — often described as *interpersonal racism.*

There is still the most common form of racism, the one we absorb by seeing, hearing and reading, a form we perceive but rarely engage with. This type of racism is termed *cultural racism* and in principle we should all be able to identify it, since it is part of the processes of everyday life. Our culture is the way we live and the traditions we follow and pass on to our children. Nevertheless, we find it difficult to accept that our everyday lives could be effected by racism because we have become so accustomed to our culture and it is difficult to see its workings. In other words it has become normal to our way of life, and we do not question our everyday experiences.

Let us take some examples of everyday processes that shape the way we — and children — see the world and are socialised by it, and see how stereotyping and racism are perpetuated.

Mass Media

By mass media in today's society, we mean the large network of communication which includes newspapers, television, radio and cinema. Since the media has the potential to reach millions of people it has an enormous capacity to shape opinion and change conceptions. As Cashmore and Troyna (1990) point out:

> Very few of us escape the media's effects; they transmit a large volume of information quickly, frequently and to large audiences. It's difficult to think of anyone besides a hermit insulating themselves from media of some sort; whether television, radio, newspaper or film. We are subjected to a steady but intense bombardment of processed information that supplies the material on which we base our view of the world.

The media is a hot-house for propagating notions that present black people as a problem or as inferior. This has important implications for the way communities with little black settlement view black people, as the media is their only source of information.

Television news reports regularly present groups of black people as a problem, as aggressors or as incompetent and unable to manage their affairs. Let us reflect on some examples as seen from the perspective of young children. All the main channels transmit the day's news reports before seven thirty in the evening. Political unrest involving black people is rarely analysed; it is more likely to be sensationalised and linked more to racial identity than to the root cause of any disturbance. The urban disturbances in the 1980s were often referred to as 'race riots' even when it was perfectly obvious that white people were involved in the so-called 'rioting'. Very little was made of the reasons why people were angry; reasons mostly to do with the unfair treatment of people from particular urban areas, with poor conditions in housing, employment and in some cases with unfair pressure from the police. In other words, the response of some inner city people to economic crisis was only translated in terms of *what* was happening and not why.

When news coverage includes reports on famine and war, black people are again presented as either mindless aggressors or passive and hopeless victims waiting for the benevolence of our government and charities to raise enough money to feed them. Children take particular note of these images because schools often help to raise money, but the schools fall into the same trap as the media by offering little explanation to children about how these situations arise. In fact the adults have often absorbed media explanations of civil war as the cause for famine, while issues of trade, third world debt and the reasons for initial poverty and political instability are largely ignored. Documentaries sometimes deal with these issues but these reach a far smaller audience. An excellent book which offers a clear exposition on some of the reasons for famine and poverty in much of our world is Nick Rowlings' *Commodities: How the World was taken to Market* (1987).

Television programmes often promote racist views or stereotypes of South Asian and African-Caribbean people and at the same time acknowledge and give credence to the view that this is a 'normal', and therefore acceptable, part of our society. Programmes such as *Till Death Us Do Part* and *EastEnders* and others featuring popular comedians such as Freddie Star, continue to perpetuate racist and sexist views. Programmes which try to deal with issues of racism more sympathetically, such as *Grange Hill* and *The Bill* often unintentionally present a caricatured picture of the way black people live and experience life in Britain today, again tending to perpetuate views of them as passive victims or aggressors. In other words, as a problem, rather than ordinary people, families and community members.

Older and newer films that are popular among children and adults but which portray overt racist images continue to be televised. Old films such as *Tarzan* or *Gone With The Wind* portray black people as savages, slaves or servants who act as inferiors, martyrs or are 'problems' to white people. Newer movies such as the Indiana Jones or Short Circuit series continue to do exactly the same, in present-day society. The popular culture of television therefore continues to promote racism, and our children continue to absorb it. Troyna and Hatcher (1992) illustrate very powerfully in their interviews with children, the effects of television on primary children's perceptions of the third world and the way they view black people and white. Three children responded as follows when asked about their ideas about black people in the third world:

> J: ..the Blacks in Africa and that think that white people are so great, they think they're brilliant because they've got all this water and food and these dead good clothes and that.

> C: Yes like in *Indiana Jones and the Last Crusade.*

> E: I think it was Princess Diana wasn't it sitting in the back once? Yes, that's it and they were all greeting them and everything and they took them to this dead nice..

> J: They were just going like that to touch the elephant. They thought the elephant was good as well because of Princess Diana. They think Whites are brilliant but a white princess.. (pp139- 140 1992)

In Troyna and Hatcher's (1992) book the children reproduced stereotyped images of white superiority and black inferiority, drawing out images of Africa as a primitive continent. When the children were asked how they knew these things, they said that they had seen it on television in Tarzan films and on the news. The authors assert that the powerful images portrayed by television of royal visits, famine relief and white intervention to 'save' black people offers a distorted and limited picture of third world countries. All of us have grown up with this distorted information.

The distortions perpetuated by television are equally true of the press and radio broadcasting. Newspaper reporting has less visual impact than television but sensationalist headlines sell newspapers. The press and radio reach a wide audience and are often equally guilty of focusing on black people only when reporting items of violence, famine, political unrest and sport. Some academics and researchers go further and have argued that issues of 'race' are not only reflected through populist understandings but also change and shape the attitudes and consciousness of the public towards black people. According to Husband (1974):

> The press has continued to project an image of Britain as a white society in which the coloured population is seen as some kind of aberration, a problem, or just an oddity (p145,1974).

Husband (1974) goes on to argue that people's attitudes toward black communities are negatively reinforced through this process. This has serious implications for white people who live in areas where few black people live, because they rely almost entirely on the media for their information about black communities. If this is largely negative then it follows that people in white areas will have a misinformed view. This confounds the notion that anti-racist and multicultural education is only relevant in multi-racial areas. On the contrary, it suggests that these approaches are even more needed in white areas.

Language

What could be more normal than human beings using language to communicate with each other? Using language is normal but we must remember that every language carries with it a range of cultural values and these are transmitted through the use of words. Languages are always developing, as our culture and way of life changes. New words are added to express new concepts, for example, the word 'yuppy' was coined to explain a group of people who were a new phenomenon created by our society. In the same way some existing words take on new meanings as our culture changes over time: 'culture', 'education', 'childhood' and 'leisure' have had different meanings attached to them at different times in the history of our language. Thus are all languages dynamic: they change over time and are influenced by economic, technological, familial and other changes to our society. Languages evolve.

English is not a 'pure' language; its origins are Germanic. English language has also been influenced by other languages and cultures, for example, the words 'bazaar', 'pyjama' and 'bungalow' come from the languages of South Asia. Closer to Britain, words such as 'cafe' and 'rendezvous' are easily recognised as having origins in French. This all sounds relatively harmless and a somewhat natural process. However, if we look at the evolution of English during Britain's imperial past and the language used to justify the oppression of particular groups of people, we will see that there is also a language of prejudice. Our culture accepts that the word 'black' denotes something negative. It is usually associated with dirt, impurity, ugliness, sadness, evil and doom. Black has been added to other words to emphasise this negative quality e.g. blackleg, blackmail, black mood, blacklist, black sheep, black day and so forth. It has become a normal part of our everyday language. We accept that if the word black is used, it is likely to denote something negative. The word 'dark' is used in the same manner, yet we continue to call Africa the 'Dark Continent' and children know that calling another person a 'blackie' is derogatory. Language is a powerful vehicle and can be used to convey negative messages about a person's skin colour.

In America in the 1960s black people recognised the fact that black was associated with ugliness and evil and some civil rights leaders such as Marcus Garvey started the 'Black is Beautiful' movement. It was out of this movement that many groups who experience racism chose to refer to themselves as black, in an effort to redefine the term as something to be linked with experience. Black is not the only word that has particular connotations. Many English dictionaries enter words such as 'nigger' as part of the stock of English words. 'Nigger' can only draw on our part in slavery, and sayings such as 'nigger in the woodpile' and 'niggardly' are still heard on television and in everyday conversation. The English language contains notoriously negative and disparaging words to describe people who are not white and English, and children hear these regularly enough to use them themselves to hurt other children. Words such as paki, yid, yanky, taffy, wop, and wog are used by adults to put other 'races' down. However, those words associated with black people still hold the most negative value, as children themselves soon learn (Kelly & Cohn, 1988).

What may appear to many as apparently innocent language may hide other prejudices. The word 'immigrant' is often used to describe people whose parents or grandparents immigrated but who are themselves born and brought up in Britain. This implies that they are in a 'host' country and therefore will at some point leave! Equally the word 'minority' suggests that a group has less than full rights, and that the 'majority' is all that matters (Birch, 1985). Other words such as 'native', 'primitive' and 'tribe' are used to describe people in other countries, but are rarely used to describe groups in England. We can relate to a group of Samoans or Maoris being described on television as engaged in 'primitive tribal' dance and dress but if the same were suggested of morris dancers, the queen's soldiers or Scottish highland dancers, many people might fly to the defence of a 'British tradition'. The fact that the dance and dress of other groups may be part of their tradition and represent a sophisticated social process is rarely discussed, because the use of words like primitive allows us to dismiss them as of no value. Racism is perpetuated through our language.

Jokes and graffiti

If we are to discuss the subliminal and everyday processes by which racism is normalised in our society these two areas deserve some consideration. Most people have seen racist graffiti and heard racist jokes and failed to take action against either. We might have felt uncomfortable, but considered it too 'normal' to warrant some kind of confrontation or action. There are very few positive images of black people in large public places or on advertising boards in our environment, but almost everyone has seen racist graffiti. Similarly racist jokes about black people, Irish people and Travellers are commonly heard and accepted as innocent fun. In fact it is commonly accepted that if you cannot take a joke (however offensive) then you are anti-social or have a chip on your shoulder. Jokes and graffiti are important indicators of what is acceptable in our society; if graffiti is offensive enough it is removed. And if it is not removed then it gives a certain message to all our children; the message that it is acceptable to be racist. Equally, jokes that degrade and humiliate certain groups are based on the view that people will find the jokes funny because they share the underlying racist assumptions and stereotypical constructs.

Art and literature

Culture in any society is learned. It contributes to the behaviour, values, attitudes and beliefs we hold. Culture, like language, is dynamic and ever-changing. Our parents pass on their culture to their children but they do it through vehicles such as language, play, art and literature. Schools and

other educational institutions extend our learning in this way through the humanities, science, the arts etc. Our culture also determines what clothes we wear, our diet, religious beliefs and relationships. Culture is much more than this, but the important point is that it is learned and that it is all around us. We need to explore how two areas of our culture, art and literature, determine how we see black people and what values, attitudes and beliefs are promoted through them and normalised from one generation to the next.

We have all read (or seen on television) some of the old stories that formed part of our childhood such as *Little Black Sambo* and *Robinson Crusoe*. Literature of this kind is often read uncritically and thus children, and adults, absorb the attitudes and values of the author without questioning them. For example, the story of Robinson Crusoe is familiar to most of us but how many of us question why Crusoe never uses 'Man Friday's' real name? Or why the labour relationship between the two men was that of master and slave, or why, even with 'Man Friday' by his side, Crusoe would bemoan his isolation and loneliness! Black people in much of our traditional and contemporary literature are portrayed stereotypically as passive, stupid, ugly or beastly. In a more hidden form the language used in children's literature to describe black people's food, dress and physique is often through words like 'strange', 'exotic', 'unusual', 'weird'. In Section 2 of this book we look at the positive strategies we can use with young children to promote a realistic and fair impression of our multiracial society.

Although there are now a few black artists, actors and theatre companies they are still not part of the mainstream but rather on the fringes. Anyway this is a recent development and most of us rely on what constituted 'arts' in our own, and our parents' past. Walking through one of our most prestigious art galleries, I recently overheard a man in his late fifties remark that if there were other civilisations, as had been suggested in a documentary he had seen on Africa and India, then why was there no evidence of their art or sculpture for the world to see? He then concluded that obviously there could not have been such civilisations because if there had we would have the evidence in the gallery. His remarks brought home to me that what is omitted is as important in portraying our culture as what we choose to transmit. Given Britain's past and lengthy relationship with South Asia and some parts of Africa and the Caribbean, the man in the gallery was right to ask his question, but unfortunately he reached the wrong conclusion because he only had his own and the gallery's limited, and biased, cultural experience to draw on.

When we go to most art galleries, or the theatre or the ballet (it is significant perhaps that these art forms are considered to be the elite transmitters of our culture) we rarely experience the work of black painters, actors or dancers. And it is through these omissions that we neglect the values of a multiracial society, and accept as normal that the arts are a white preserve. In more popular culture such as sport, pop music, jazz and contemporary dance there is much better representation of our multiracial society. It is important for us to look at the older classical forms of our art and literature much more critically, and to challenge some of the hidden as well as overt assumptions about black people's ability to contribute to these — still highly valued — forms today.

SECTION II
Towards Good Practice

CHAPTER 3

Language, Learning and Multilingual Development

How important is language?

Language is the most powerful tool in the development of any human being. It is undeniably the greatest asset we possess. A good grasp of language is synonymous with a sound ability to think. In other words language and thought are inseparable (Vygotsky, 1986).

Knowing language means we automatically know grammar. It also means that we have a system and structure of thought. For young children the acquisition of their first language and its development depend primarily on the role that adults play in their interactions with the child, and on the type of environment and play situations available. But language is even more than this. It is through the language or languages that we speak that we form a sense of identity, community and belonging. The way the languages we speak are perceived also influences the way we feel about ourselves.

Language is as much a matter of passion as cultural identity. When some Scottish people argue for national independence for Scotland they often cite the differences between themselves and the English, and inevitably they cite that they possess a different culture and language. The

Welsh and Irish have used the same ethnic arguments. We can also see from some of the conflict following the demise of the Soviet Union and the Eastern European struggle to achieve democracy, that language played a strong role in people's arguments for separate nation states.

Language development and young children

As every early years worker knows, language development needs to be taken seriously from birth. Yet most of the literature on early learning appears to focus solely on linguistic development from the age of three and upwards. This is a great mistake, because if we attempt to understand and know more about language development from birth onward we are more likely to understand and work more effectively with under-threes and their families. It is important to understand how babies, toddlers and infants acquire language so that we can assist the development of bilingualism in the same way.

☐ **0-6 months:** — No baby is too young to talk to. Babies recognise sound and are attentive to adult voices. They can be soothed or disturbed by sounds of differing rhythms and pitch. Parents and carers should talk to babies and from experience they will learn that very young babies respond well to voices. Babies also enjoy the sound of singing and music and find low rhythmic sounds particularly soothing.

As the baby develops it will pay more attention to non-verbal adult behaviour. Individual attention which engages directly and closely to the baby often yields smiles and babbles. Adults should continue to talk, smile and engage non-verbally through pleasant facial expressions while looking directly at the baby's face. According to Clarke (1992), babies will try to imitate and respond to adult voices and will respond well to looking into a mirror. She advises fixing baby mirrors to a wall at the baby's sitting height or providing baby mirrors in strong plastic frames.

☐ **6-12 months:** — babies at this age can respond in a number of ways to language, they can initiate communication which is still mainly non-verbal or involves the imitation of sounds. Most babies respond to their names and to simple directives, for example, to wave good-bye to someone. Adults should encourage children's language development by playing simple games and using rhymes, such as, ' Incy, Wincy Spider', ' Peek-a-boo' and 'Five Little Frogs'. Nursery rhymes and songs with bodily actions are particularly enjoyable for all young children.

If you have parents from a mixture of ethnic backgrounds ask them to bring in simple rhymes and songs or the equivalent of the English ones where the actions can remain familiar, a good example of this is Hickory, Dickory Dock. The Urdu (spoken by many Pakistani families) equivalent is called Chuha, Chuha, Cha-cha. A compilation of taped or transliterated (written in English script) rhymes and songs is a very useful resource.

Babies of this age should also be encouraged to respond to simple directives, such as; *'Here's your biscuit'*, *'Take the bottle'*, *'Wave your hand'*. Carers can encourage babies by imitating the sounds they make, and even at this age it is important to tell stories. Preferably this should be done using objects that are familiar to the baby like the dolls or plastic animals the baby plays with.

☐ **1-2 years:** — Rouse and Griffin (1992) argue that very young children, and especially those under two need a responsive and loving adult to engage with on a regular basis. They assert that showering a child in language, but without the close relationship with a 'significant' adult would be unhelpful. As they say:

If this were sufficient, it would be enough to settle a two year old in front of the television or with his (sic) own sack of taped stories. However, quality experiences which support children's language development need to be reciprocal exchanges; responses should follow the pattern, tone and nature of the children's communication. (p143, 1992)

In an ethnically diverse setting this is even more pertinent, because there may be cross-cultural considerations. Rouse and Griffin (1992) supply an appropriate example of this. On their visit to a nursery school for 0-6 year olds in Bologna, Italy, they found educators in the baby unit giving different attention to a Chinese baby who had initially caused them some concern. Apparently, in the initial stages of transition from home to nursery the baby had cried constantly and clung to the mother. The nursery staff had taken several steps to accommodate the baby, mainly by changing their own behaviour due to their careful observation and subsequent assessment of the situation.

They took three significant steps: Firstly, by observing and copying the way the Chinese mother carried her baby on her hip with the baby's legs astride and arms around the adult. Secondly, the educators had observed the distressing effects on the baby on hearing the unfamiliar intonation when Italian was spoken. The educators took to imitating Chinese language sounds which the baby found comforting and familiar. Thirdly, the educators were able to encourage the baby's father to make some tapes on which he sang lullabies. This too proved to be successful at siesta time for the Chinese baby and to the other children as part of their language awareness education. This is an excellent example of good practice. Had the staff not been able to utilise their observation skills effectively or been insensitive to cross-cultural communication and child-rearing practices the Chinese child would certainly have suffered negative effects.

Between the ages of one and two the child makes a great deal of linguistic progress. Children develop from uttering single words, or their beginnings, and using sounds reflecting syllables to make meaningless words and sentences, to using complete sentences. They enjoy and engage with simple stories, rhymes, songs and jingles. Adults should read to children of this age and engage in 'active' listening when they are trying to communicate. This means not just listening with our ears but also visibly engaging with the child's gaze and making non-verbal and verbal signs that we are hearing what the child is saying. Children of this age enjoy playing as much with toys that make sounds as they do making a variety of sounds themselves. They enjoy playing with their growing competence and confidence with language.

Adults should continue to give simple directives but also extend this to asking simple questions, giving explanations, extending the child's short sentences and introducing new vocabulary, for example, the names of objects in the home or parts of the body. Although toddlers still need a lot of rest and sleep, they are also very physically active and need toys and activities which will extend their physical development. Games and movement to music and rhymes should be a regular event.

As children develop adults should continue to read to them, preferably while the child is seated on the adult's lap. Books and simple puzzles should always be available for play.

☐ **2-3 year olds:** — children of this age are rapidly acquiring vocabulary. They develop from speaking in short sentences to longer ones and from using descriptive and 'doing' words to including pronouns such as: me, you, he and I. They still find it easier to talk about the here and now, the present rather than the past or future. During play children of this age can be observed talking to themselves and using more complete sentences. They do however, still continue to play with sounds and make up meaningless utterances.

Physically, children at this age are very active and developing rapidly in their gross and small motor movements. Adults should help children understand the concept of a book. This can be done by identifying the names given to different parts of the book, such as, the pages, the cover, pictures and words. Apart from reading to children and using their favourite stories we can help children to make their own picture books using, for example, their holiday photographs. This will help encourage the development of a lifelong love for stories and reading.

Children of this age often mispronounce words; adults should use these words often in a variety of contexts for imitation by the child. Adults should not constantly correct the child's speech. This is a stage when carers should attempt to engage in lengthier and more sustained conversation with children. Two year olds continue to enjoy games, puzzles, rhymes, songs and music activities. If the child is interested in making marks on paper and engaging in construction activities this should be encouraged, and all efforts praised.

Many educators are also familiar with the fact that children in this age group have learned to use contractions (Clarke, 1992) such as: isn't, can't and won't and that they will readily use them! It is important the we reason with children using clear, simple and meaningful sentences. Children whose mother tongue is not English require a great deal more visual and auditory cues when listening to stories in English and all children need to hear a variety of languages through rhymes, songs and short stories.

☐ **3-5 year olds:** — During this age phase children are becoming much more self-reliant, they want to attempt to do things for themselves. This should be encouraged in the early years setting. Not just in relation to personal tasks such as toiletting or dressing, but also in consideration of others and in sharing tasks. Social responsibilities

such as handing out the milk or helping to tidy up after activities is couched in new language experiences. The way adults give explanations can have more meaning to the child than the adult intended. For example, the adult who praises every child for finishing her milk or eating all her fruit is indirectly criticising the children who cannot finish their snack. After all, there is nothing particularly wonderful about finishing every snack that we are given!

Although most children are constructing more complex sentences and articulating past and future tenses using more vocabulary, adults must be careful not to assume that the style of speech between the home and early childhood setting will be, or should be, the same. Considerable thought and empathy needs to be shown by educators when making requests: for example, a child who is asked to do things through short commands such as, 'Sit down' or 'Eat your dinner' may not at first understand an educator's requests framed as follows: 'Shall we all sit down?' or 'Would you like to eat your dinner?' The child may perceive these as genuine questions to which she has a choice and her response may well be 'No'! We need to be aware that children come from a range of linguistic experiences and that educators are in a unique position to develop language, if initially we listen and observe and then build on what the child already knows.

Most children also begin to take an interest in learning numbers. Their understanding varies depending on their experience. Some may be able to say numbers in sequence but not know what this means. Their grammar and articulation skills are improving but they still make mistakes. It is vital that at this age children get plenty of first hand experiences through everyday activities such as laying a table or cooking with an adult. Talking through these activities is the key to developing language. Counting provides a basis for developing a range of mathematical skills.

The excitement and talk generated by a visit to the grocer or to look at how many round things, say, can be seen, can be marred by an adult who does not give the young child enough time to express herself. Going over the events of a trip, a cooking activity, a story or discussing the content of a child's painting can encourage children to engage in sustained dialogue which is meaningful and interesting to them.

☐ **5-7 year olds:** — there is a very wide range of developmental difference in language skills at this age, largely depending on the experiences a child has had in the first five years. Donaldson, in her seminal work *Children's Minds* (1978), shows how early years educators adhering strictly to Piaget's developmental stages in order to consolidate children's learning could limit the development of some children. Both Vygotsky (1986) and Donaldson (1978) put much greater emphasis on educators entering the child's social world to build on her learning. More recently Donaldson's (1992) work on *Human Minds* also stresses the importance of the emotional factor in learning.

This means that we first need to assess what children can do, and then give them contexts that are meaningful to their social, emotional, cultural and linguistic experiences. As Bernstein (1970) put it, 'If the culture of the teacher is to become part of the consciousness of the child, then the culture of the child must first be in the consciousness of the teacher'

To a large extent, for this age group, play is still a very important vehicle through which language develops, but educators are constrained by the school national curriculum. Not so much because of the content but more the breadth of experiences educators are required to cover, as well as poor resourcing, both human and material.

In this age group there is usually a rapid increase in vocabulary, longer and more complex sentences and fewer mistakes. Most children learn to read and write and need plenty of extension work to their listening and talking skills. Children should be encouraged to read every day and certainly need to be read to. For the younger ones in the age group the use of puppets and flannel boards with cut-out characters from favourite story books can allow them to retell stories.

The use of language in problem solving activities and the development of more varied use of language such as prediction and evaluation should be developed. Science, maths and technology are excellent areas of school work to encourage this type of language and thought through the use of practical activities.

Children are naturally inquisitive and will need to explore the wide range of books and their purposes. Access to a book area and a library containing story, information, specialist and reference books should be available and widely used. The older children can be encouraged to use dictionaries. All children still enjoy singing and music. Drama should be used to extend language activities. Children's writing takes a greater focus in these years and an awareness of writing for a range of audiences should be encouraged.

Most of all children should have the opportunity to discuss their work with each other and regularly with an adult. Talking about aspects of a story or their creative writing or an experiment helps children to think through and consolidate their learning, just as adults need to. To collaborate with each other and share ideas does not come naturally to children and the skills to do this should be taught gradually.

Children also show a growing awareness of other languages and their attention should be drawn to a range of languages and in particular community languages. This will be dealt with later in this chapter.

Language Development Versus Linguistic Prejudice and Racism

We are often led to believe (particularly by politicians) that the standardised form of English is, and was, always part of the English heritage. This is completely untrue. English, like all other languages was standardised over time and has evolved from its Germanic roots with the influence of many other languages on the way. There are two main views on the English language:

☐ The cultural heritage view — those who hold this view believe:

— *that the English language is fixed and unchanging;*

— *that there was a golden age (probably the 1930s — 1950s) when those who mattered in society held a consensus on a particular type of English;*

— *that standards of English in society should be mirrored by those in the Universities of Cambridge and Oxford, the Times newspaper and Public schools;*

— *that accents, dialects, Creoles and Patois should not be reflected in our culture through literature, theatre or television because this may affect the purity of the English language;*

— *that written English should have higher status than spoken English.*

☐ The cultural analysis view — those who hold this view believe:

— *that society is dynamic and ever changing, and so is language;*

— *that diversity in language, such as accents, does not threaten standard forms of English;*

— *that all children have a right to learn standard English for future empowerment in the workplace and for public writing because it is the language of power in our society;*

— *that literature reflects our changing times and experiences and therefore what constitutes 'good' literature will reflect the change;*

— *that talking and listening skills are crucial.*

Those who hold the cultural heritage view of English are likely to view ethnic minority languages with prejudice and to want children to lose their links with their mother tongue and to assimilate with the English speaking group. Just as there is a hierarchy of valuing some racial groups more than others, there is a similar racism towards languages. We need to move towards the cultural analysis view of the place and role of English, in order to free ourselves from such prejudice and work positively with children.

Recent research by Rudolph Schaffer and his team, Ogilvy et al (1991) in Scotland have shown how children in multi-ethnic Scottish nurseries are treated differently, according to their ethnicity, by nursery staff. The research reports that all nursery staff felt they treated the children according to their individual needs. However, when observations and video tapes of interactions between staff and children were analysed the findings were disturbing. Although the staff felt they were giving equal and caring attention to all the children, they were in reality favouring the indigenous Scottish group.

The South Asian children were reported to be receiving less attention, fewer verbal interactions and staff used poor models of English when explaining things to them. In fact, staff often failed to attempt sustained conversations with the minority group and spoke for the children when answers were required. They resorted to a 'pidgin' English, so providing a distorted version of English to the very children who most needed correct models. The findings of this research came as a surprise to the staff concerned because they, like so many others, are oblivious to their lack of knowledge and training in the area of multilingual support and the particular needs of those children learning English as their second or third language. Staff find themselves falling back on the knowledge they do possess, which is usually limited and learned within prejudiced frameworks.

It is interesting to note that research done in the Netherlands by Verhallen et al (1989) elicited similar findings. Most European countries with ethnic minorities are beginning to identify the lack of understanding by educators of the support needed by children and the training required for multilingual settings, as the major factors in underachievement amongst ethnic minority and black children. At the end of the day there is no excuse for causing cognitive failure among children on such a large scale. The research by Biggs and Edwards (1992) is yet another depressing reminder that children in some infant schools continue to be grossly disadvantaged by their educators.

In their paper entitled: *'I treat them all the same'; teacher-pupil talk in multiethnic classrooms*, Biggs and Edwards analyse data which was collected systematically using both quantitative and qualitative methods. They sum up their findings as follow:

> The underachievement of ethnic minority children continues to be an issue for educators in many parts of the world. Attempts to explain and remedy the underachievement have been many and varied. Recent discussions, however, have focused increasingly on the notion of institutional racism and a number of commentators have tried to identify the ways in which the assumptions and practices of the dominant

group work to the detriment of minority children in the classroom. (p161,1992).

Their research goes on to describe their investigation of the interactions of five different teachers in multi-ethnic infant classes of Year One children. As they report,

Teachers were found to interact less frequently with Black children than White; they have fewer exchanges lasting more than thirty seconds with Black children; they also spent less time with them discussing the particular task which had been set...It is suggested that there is an urgent need for teachers and teacher educators to look more critically at the ways in which stereotypes are mediated through language (p163,1992).

Young children need to have their languages valued and their home experiences affirmed in order to feel secure enough to venture into the language and culture of their early years setting. The staff need training, knowledge and guidance on the development of appropriate bilingual programmes.

Bilingual and Multilingual Children

'I'm not putting my wellies in that bag, it's got Paki writing on it!'

The statement was uttered by 3½ year old Amar. When I asked him how he knew it was Urdu script he promptly turned to another plastic bag with English writing on and said, 'Look, this one's English it goes like this (he made zig-zag movements with one finger from left to right) and this one with the 'Paki' writing goes like this (making circular movements in the air with his finger from right to left) see!!' His defiant expression had melted to a smug smile at my apparent ignorance of the comparative status of these two languages.

The nursery class where this took place had very caring staff and was in the process of developing some very good practice for bilingual support. Nevertheless Amar was quite capable, as he so aptly illustrated, of not only identifying print but differentiating between the scripts and allocating quite clearly their relative status. That is, anything to do with Urdu (Amar's home language) was not to be associated with outside of the home. The implications of such incidents — and this is by no means an isolated example — raise many issues for those of us concerned with the education and care of young children.

Young children are a product of their environment. Both the hidden and overt messages which pervade our society are brought into the early years setting and educators need to equip themselves to deal with any false generalisations which the children in their charge may voice. If children absorb negative messages about their home language from others this will inevitably affect their self-image and may even foster negative feelings about their family background. What their educators think and do in this area is of vital importance. Monolingual and multilingual educators have a vital role to play in supporting children's home languages and developing positive attitudes in all children about being bilingual.

What is this thing called bilingualism or multilingualism?

Over 70% of the world's population has more than one language. However in British education and care systems being bilingual is still too often perceived as an aberration, or worse, as something children should grow out of. This of course prevents bilingual children's total linguistic ability from being highlighted as something positive and as a resource. Too often bilingual children are perceived as being merely non-English speakers; they are perceived as a problem. Research directly contradicts this view, showing that supporting a child's home language aids the development of English learning and conceptual growth (Verhallen et al 1989; Cummins, 1984; Pinsent, 1992) in other words, a strong foundation in the child's home language is a necessary prerequisite to the learning of a second or third language.

Research from Scandinavia, Canada and America has demonstrated this but in the UK there is a paucity of research in this whole area. British governments have been unwilling to take the needs of bilinguals very seriously. One of the few projects carried out in the UK was funded by the European Community. Evidence from this MOTET project in Bradford (Fitzpatrick, 1987) showed that Panjabi and English speaking bilinguals performed better in English and other areas of the curriculum when they were given the opportunity to use their home language and be taught using their home language simultaneously with English.

It might be thought that for children to be bilingual they would have to have equal proficiency in two languages. This is an inadequate definition because most of the world's bilinguals would not qualify for this category! A much more appropriate definition of bilingual children would be to so describe those who use more than one language regularly and effectively in their particular language communities. The extent to which children are able to control and manage their languages, depends on where they live and who they use which language with. This in turn will be affected by the age of the child, whether the languages are learnt at the same time and whether they are given different value.

Many young children from ethnic minority backgrounds will be at a variety of levels in the languages they experience. For example, many Pakistani children might use Panjabi as their mother tongue but Urdu as their formal language and be introduced to Arabic as their religious language. These children would also be familiar with some English through their immediate environment e.g. watching television, going shopping or hearing others speak English. This language experience has a profound effect upon the child's perceptions. Many of our children are multilingual and not just bilingual. However, as the child has more contact with the outside world through early education, care and school there is pressure from parents and educators for the child to acquire English because it is the official language and therefore the language of empowerment.

It is in the child's interest that she acquires English as a second (or third, or fourth) language in the most efficient and effective way, without prejudice to the home languages. Educators should be able to provide a carefully planned programme of bilingual support. Having bilingual educators makes this task considerably easier. For monolingual educators, the following provides a starting point for evaluating the possibility of offering appropriate bilingual support:

☐ What efforts have been made to check the attitudes of educators toward children's ethnicity and home languages?

☐ What training has taken place on understanding racism in British society and in particular linguistic racism?

☐ What procedures, records or assessments are available to measure a child's competence in her home language and English?

☐ What do we know about the children's cultures and language experiences which could help in the acquisition of English and the support of the home language and culture?

Answers to these questions and a programme of training to develop appropriate concepts, knowledge, attitudes and skills are essential if educators seriously wish to develop effective English as a second language (E2L) teaching and support strategies.

When we look at the task which faces the children who are to become fluent bilinguals it is clear that we should give them every support. Priscilla Clarke (1992) working in a very multilingual society in Australia, cites the Ministry of Education (p9, 1987) to show what a huge task children face in the process of learning another language. Rightly, Clarke is keen to point out the parallels between acquiring the first language and subsequent languages. According to the Australian Ministry of Education, the second language learner must achieve the following in order to acquire a new language:

☐ A new set of sounds and sound groupings, which may or may not be like those in the first language.

☐ New intonation patterns and their meanings and new patterns of stress and pause. These are rarely available in written form.

☐ A new script or alphabet.

☐ A new set of sound-symbol relationships and spelling.

☐ New vocabulary.

☐ New ways of putting words together (a new grammar) and organising information and communication.

☐ New non-verbal signals, and new meanings for old non-verbal signals.

☐ New social signals and new ways of getting things done through language.

☐ New rules about the appropriateness of language for specific situations and roles.

☐ New sets of culturally specific knowledge, values and behaviour.

☐ A new culturally specific view of the world.

☐ An ability to relate to people and to express feelings and emotions in the new language.(Ministry of Education, 1987, p.9 from Clarke, 1992)

Monolingual educators and bilingual children — a contradiction in terms?

The kind of experiences offered to our young children reflect the degree of commitment we have to supporting bilingualism. Monolingual educators in particular need to feel that they have an important role to play if they wish to promote their children's familial, cultural, religious, social and cognitive development (Swann Report, 1985; Children Act, 1989). There is always a difference between a child's home and school language, a cultural difference for all. Supporting bilingualism is simply an extension of good practice in language acquisition and development.

For a young child, learning another language is no different to learning their first language. Bilingual children should therefore not be withdrawn from the mainstream settings or classes, since this is precisely where an educator would expect to find the richest and most natural models of spoken English. Monolingual educators can adopt some of the following practices to support bilingual children:

☐ Educators can adopt a positive attitude to all children's languages by positively recognising the linguistic diversity within English and extending this good practice by also valuing and building on any other language a child may have.

☐ Language issues should be seen in the context of education for racial equality and local education authority language centre resources can often be used to raise the awareness of staff and monolingual children.

☐ Formative profile language records based on regular discussion with parents and observation of children's use of language should be kept, updated and consulted regularly.

☐ Parents should be involved, informing them as far as possible about their children's education. Promoting parental understanding of bilingualism and cultural diversity helps to broaden the experiences of everyone interacting with young children, as well as dispelling negative or prejudiced views based upon ignorance. Bilingual parents, relatives, community members and secondary school pupils can help educators support bilingual pupils.

☐ Bilingual children should be encouraged to speak in their home language with other bilinguals. This also aids language awareness for monolingual children: through exploring and discussing their questions an educator can help to dispel false generalisations about languages other than English.

☐ Educators can begin to learn words and phrases of their children's home languages. This not only serves the local community well but it can also be immensely reassuring and offer security to a young child who may be in distress in an unfamiliar setting. It helps conceptual understanding and can be fun! Learning about our children's community languages, cultures and customs helps educators to provide a more appropriate and relevant curriculum.

☐ As far as possible bilingual children's learning should take place and be supported in the normal class setting, that is, working with their English first language peers. This is where the most natural models of language are uttered and learned.

☐ The recognition and use of the child's home language by the educator and supported with additional auditory, visual and tactile cues is vital. Bilingual stories, rhymes and songs should be learned or taped and used regularly. Bilingual tapes can be made by members of the local community or secondary school pupils can be bought. These can be used with extra support such as sound effects and puppets. Simple story books can be transliterated and told bilingually by any educator. Photographs and pictures can also be valuable resources when transliterations are included for the use of the educator.

Creating a multilingual ethos

A bilingual classroom can be an exciting and enjoyable experience for all young children. Educators need to consider the hidden messages their classroom environment and practices transmit to the community that they serve. An atmosphere should be created where ethnic minority parents feel comfortable to come and interact with the children and their educators. Home-school links are vital to this endeavour and can be promoted in a number of ways. Parents should have access to information about their child. Letters should be translated and efforts made to use interpreters with parents who are still learning English.

Educators can create a language-rich environment based on the parents' and children's diverse cultural backgrounds. Bilingual signs should be displayed around the classroom and outside it. Dual language books and tapes should be displayed where they are easily accessible. Use can be made of a variety of multicultural resources offering positive images through such things as posters, play utensils, dolls, games, puzzles and music tapes. The curriculum on offer should also incorporate a variety of festivals, family life and art and craft materials. If the classroom resources and curriculum reflect the children's lives they are more likely to want to engage in and learn from the activities we provide.

Staff checklist for creating multilingual support in the early years.

☐ *Induction:* How are children and their parents introduced to your particular early years setting? Whether children come from a working class background (most early years settings are framed in middle class language) or a home where English is not the first language, we must ask ourselves how the children might feel in their first few days. First impressions are as important to children as they are to their families and the adults who work in the setting.

Children need to feel they can trust and rely on the adults around them. Each child will be bringing her unique experience to the new environment, and this might include issues of family stability, whether the child was born in Britain or recently arrived, and individual personality shaped by her every-day carer within the family or outside. If educators are able to glean information of this nature from the family they can support the child appropriately.

Children will be able to form relationships more easily with adults who create a warm and loving environment. Adults who are caring, patient and take a regular and genuine interest in the child will help children to feel secure, confident and positive about themselves. Children should hear their home language spoken in their early years setting in the first few days at least. This can be facilitated by ensuring that parents are clear that you want them to stay with their child for part of the day with an educator. During this time the parents should speak to their children in the home language. This creates familiarity, values the home language and shows the parents that you respect their community.

If it is at all possible it would also help if educators learnt some words and useful sentences to help children feel secure. Greetings in the child's home language immediately set a happy tone from the beginning. Practical words related to feeding, toileting, dressing and praising can easily be learnt or transliterated into an exercise book for regular reference.

Best of all, early years settings should employ bilingual staff or/and encourage ethnic minority and black parents and community members to train for working in the early years. Children need to see role models like themselves and ideally have the right to learn through their home language whilst they are acquiring English.

Traditionally most people have only associated English as a second language with the South Asian communities. We must remember that many African-Caribbean families are bilingual too and that their so-called 'Creoles' are not subverted forms of English. Children from these communities also need to have their English acquisition monitored very carefully. Unless we ask all parents about their language heritage many other communities: Jewish, Polish, Greek, Lithuanian etc. might not reveal their multilingual identity or skills

The curriculum should also reflect an anti-racist and multilingual early years environment. This will be dealt with in more detail in the next chapter.

☐ *Understanding*: do all the educators understand why children in the early stages of English acquisition may be silent or make errors? No child enters an early years setting without any experience of the English language. Although children may appear to have no spoken English they will have been exposed to English every day through the television and through their experiences of shopping, going to the doctor or dentist and in many cases through hearing other siblings and their parents speaking in English with each other or with other English speakers. Those of us with a smattering of French or some other language will know that it is sometimes easier to understand words and sentences spoken by others and more difficult to construct them for ourselves! For most young children comprehension in English precedes the spoken word. This is known as the 'silent' period.

However, some people mistake ethnic minority children's silence in the initial stages of learning English for total lack of understanding in English or, worse, as a sign that cognitive ability is lacking. Sadly, early years educators in schools and other settings can still be heard describing children in their 'silent' period as having 'no language'! Others have used the 'silent' period as an excuse for not giving ethnic minority children the time and specific tasks they need to become fluent English speakers. In other words, some educators ignore quiet children, using the 'silent' period they go through as an excuse for doing nothing for them! In fact the opposite treatment is needed: they should be showering the children with bilingual support and extra attention in English learning during every-day activities.

Educators should not try to force children to speak English during their 'silent' period, but they should provide plenty of opportunities and activities to allow the children to participate without having to speak. This should take place in the everyday learning environment which all the children inhabit. Each potential bilingual will take a different length of time to speak English because each child's experiences are different.

Clarke (1992) cites ten ways to encourage the participation of children during their 'silent' period. She recommends:

1. *Continued talking even when children do not respond.*

2. *Persistent inclusion in small groups with other children.*

3. *Use of varied questions.*

4. *Inclusion of other children as the focus in the conversation.*

5. *Use the first language.*

6. *Acceptance of non-verbal responses.*

7. *Praising of minimal effort.*

8. *Expectations to respond with repeated words and/or counting.*

9. *Structuring of programme to encourage child to child interaction.*

> *10. Provide activities which reinforce language practice through role play.*
>
> (Clarke, 1992, pp17-18)

When children do acquire the confidence and skills to begin to attempt to speak English it must be permissible, and seen as natural, that they make mistakes and errors of speech. Each error alerts educators to the problems in each child's acquisition of English. For example, children whose first language is Hindi, Urdu or Panjabi may be heard making similar mistakes, such as; *'I will shut door'*. It is not surprising that they omit the article (in this case 'the') before words such as door, because as a direct translation from the home language it makes sense — most South Asian languages do not use articles.

If educators make efforts to identify some of these patterns by learning more about the structure of the most prevalent ethnic minority languages in their community, they can help by taking appropriate strategies to language teaching. In the example cited, educators with children from South Asian backgrounds should stress the article with the words they teach, for instance children could learn about parts of their body as the head, an arm, a leg and the mouth, rather than head, arm, leg and mouth. Written labels could also reflect this principle.

Children will also use grammatical rules inappropriately. For example, saying *'I goed'* instead of *'I went'* can tell us that a child is applying the rules of changing tense but in the wrong form. Observing and listening carefully can allow educators to plan for the child to hear correct forms of English. Instant use of the correct form by the educator may be appropriate at times, for instance, a child who rushes into playgroup and says, *'I want tell story!'* to the playgroup leader could be answered with, *'You want to tell a story? Would you like to tell your story to everyone?'* In this way the child is 'given' the correct model of English without overt correction, not forcing the child to repeat or feel ashamed of her spoken English.

In infant schools some teachers may feel that national curriculum English requires them to encourage children to use standard forms of English from the beginning. This would be very damaging to children learning English as a second language. Not only will it severely knock their confidence, they will also be reluctant to speak and so lose out on interactions during activities which are vital to conceptual development.

Where possible children should still be receiving tuition and conversation in their home language.

☐ *Communicating with bilingual children?* — What strategy does your setting have? It is obvious that setting children concrete and practical activities in the normal day-to-day timetable with plenty of opportunities to listen to natural models of English, will help their second language acquisition. Nonetheless, all children still require some conceptual challenge and the opportunity to continue learning in a language they understand. A key aim for any setting should be to employ educators or helpers with the same linguistic background as the children. This may be impossible in groups where ten or more languages are represented, but even so the main community languages could be targeted for a start.

Parents are an obvious source of support and if you can encourage them to contribute their valuable skills everyone should benefit. Parents should not be unduly pressured or exploited as unpaid educators, but respect and genuine interest in their skills might well yield rewards on both sides. Parents can read stories and help out with activities, particularly those needing explanation and concept-building such as cooking or science activities. If the parents are literate they can assist with making labels, helping staff with transliteration of key words. For instance, during a topic on food or harvest, they could write the names of various fruits and foods on the back of picture flashcards, to be used by the monolingual staff when the parents are not available. A Japanese mother working with her child in a reception class produced this story 'The Beautiful Rainbow' after considerable discussion, laughter, joy and, later, pride when the story was shared with the whole class (see pp.57-58).

Secondary school children can offer a tremendous amount if their input is carefully managed. Some may be available to help during work experience while others might work from their school, devising resources. If you work in a multi-ethnic early years setting the chances are that you will have a secondary school nearby reflecting the ethnic symmetry. You can request the help of school pupils with similar cultural and linguistic backgrounds to the children.

During the development of bilingual programmes in Berkshire nurseries, some teachers decided to work on the creation of bilingual story

The beautiful rainbow

Kipper visited an old castle in Wales with his family. As it had been raining, the river near the castle became muddy.

美しい 虹

キッパーは 家族と一緒に ウェールズの古い お城へ行きました。
雨が降り続いていたので、お城の近くの川は 濁っていました。

0

After it stopped raining, Kipper found a rainbow in the sky.

雨がやんだ後 キッパーは 空に
虹を見つけました

Only one fish could be seen in the river

川には たった一匹の思、しか
見えませんでした

2

The old castle was made of rainbow-coloured stones

The rainbow was beautiful in the morning sun

3

57

古い お城は 虹色の石で
作られていた。

Kipper ate a strawberry
under the rainbow ⁴

キッパーは 虹の下で いちごを
食べました。

There was a big apple tree ⁶
nearby and some apples
dropped

近くに 大きな りんごの木があって
りんごがいくつか落ちてきました。

虹は 朝日に 映えて とても
美しいです

Kipper played with Chip ⁵
under the rainbow.

キッパーは 虹の下で チップと
遊びました。

Kipper felt happy under ⁷
the beautiful rainbow

キッパーは 美しい 虹の下で
幸せな気持ちになりました。

tapes in English and the home languages of the nursery children's favourite stories. Secondary school teachers of English devised a project, as part of their GCSE work for their pupils, to make bilingual cassette tapes. The secondary school students started by listening to tapes the teachers had made and were very critical! They reported that the teachers sounded patronising, that they all had middle class voices and that they sounded boring! They thought they could do much better.

This project produced a bank of bilingual story tapes in Panjabi, Urdu, Cantonese, Jamaican, Polish and several other languages. The secondary school students used the children's favourite books, such as: *The Tiger Who Came to Tea, Not Now Bernard, Dear Zoo* and the *Spot* books. They did this because the dual language books usually had stories targeted at older children, and some of them were not so interesting to nursery children. Each tape had sound effects and special sounds to indicate the turning of a page and each tape ended with open-ended extension questions which encouraged the children to recall aspects of the story. The tapes also represented a range of accents (mostly local), male and female voices and sometimes more than one story-teller.

The teachers made puppets and cut-out characters for the flannel board to further aid the understanding of the stories for the children. These tapes became an invaluable source for the nurseries because:

— monolingual teachers could use the tapes without the assistance or presence of a bilingual educator or helper;

— the audio (sound effects) and visual (puppets and cut-out figures) cues delighted the children, kept their attention and helped them to follow the story.

— children were increasingly found retelling the story either in their home language or English at the flannel board or during painting.

— all the children loved the stories, and those children with English as their first language who had exhibited poor language acquisition and listening skills appeared to progress as well as the bilingual children.

I can recall a four year old boy called Jamie asking me to tell the story on a particular day at story time. I reassured him that I would do so, after outdoor play had finished. He hesitated, and then asked if I could read the story 'in my mouth'. It was only after he had gone out to play that I realised

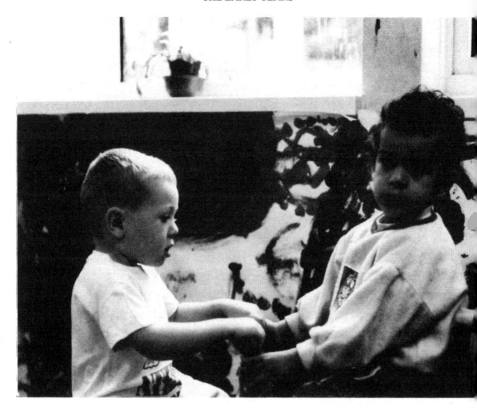

that Jamie had been trying to explain the word 'language' without knowing the actual word. The wonderful thing was that Jamie had the concept.
Language awareness of a multilingual society is of the utmost importance
to all children. Jamie was not bilingual — he wanted to hear a bilingual
story because it was enjoyable.

Other community members can also help to provide bilingual support.
Many children come from extended families where grandparents play a
key role in their care. Again, our first aim should be to encourage
African-Caribbean, South Asian and other ethnic minority community
members to become valued as educators of young children.

CHAPTER 4

Creating a Curriculum and Ethos for Racial Equality

What is education for?

When educators find themselves discussing the needs of young children in a multi-ethnic society, they often confront some of the most fundamental questions about the purpose and nature of education: *'Why educate children?'*: *'What are our priorities?'*: *'Who or what are we educating them for?'* and: *'Whose values should underpin our work?'*

I have heard these questions voiced more times than I care to remember, during training sessions with childminders, playgroup leaders, nursery workers and teachers. An anonymous letter written by a Nazi concentration camp survivor is often cited to remind us powerfully that education based on skills, knowledge and indoctrination but without regard to values, attitudes and the exploration of similarities and difference can harm whole societies:

Dear teacher,

I am the survivor of a concentration camp. My eyes saw what no man should witness: Gas chambers built by learned engineers. Children poisoned by educated physicians. Infants killed by trained nurses. Women and babies shot and burned by high school graduates.

So I am suspicious of education.

My request is: help your students become human. Your efforts must never produce learned monsters, skilled psychopaths, educated Reichmans.

Reading, writing, arithmetic are only important if they serve to make our children more human.

At the time of writing this book it is pertinent to reflect on the conditions created for children (and adults) by the war in the former Yugoslavia and the racist desire of one group to use any means, however cruel and irrational, in their inhumane pursuit of 'ethnic cleansing'. The plight of the victims reaches our newspapers and hits our television screens with stories of torture, starvation, homelessness, rape and murder. How will world history judge this human catastrophe? What do children watching the television make of these stories? We should want our children, today and in future generations, to question injustice, intolerance and notions of cultural superiority. We need to start and to sustain that process as early as possible.

In order to plan for learning we need to scrutinise our curriculum for racial bias and aim to integrate conceptual development in the areas of diversity and justice. But first of all there needs to be some sort of definition within each early years setting of what constitutes a curriculum and how we perceive children.

The definition of curriculum outlined by Hazareesingh, Simms and Anderson (1989) is a broad one, and therefore a useful starting point or working definition until educators can resolve a workable definition specific to each setting. As Hazareesingh et al assert, the curriculum can be seen as:

the sum total of experiences that the child discovers within the learning environment, including both the planned and the 'hidden curriculum', i.e., the quality of the play environment, teacher/carer styles, values and expectations, relationships between children (p35, 1989).

They also argue that early learning is essentially 'holistic' and that the young, developing child needs educators to create an environment suitable for the development of cognitive, social, emotional, aesthetic, linguistic/communicative and physical dimensions.

How we define childhood is also important. Tina Bruce (1987), drawing on the theories of Froebel, Montessori and other influential early childhood educators, emphasises that childhood should be seen as a valid part of life and not just as a preparation or training for adulthood. The Early Years Curriculum Group (1992) state that young children learn from everything that they experience in their environment, from everything that happens to them. They do not compartmentalise their learning into subjects.

If the child's environment is racist and sexist she will learn this as something acceptable to the 'significant' adults around her, and this is certainly the case presently in most British contexts. Children learn from their environments like sponges soak up water. They are the image of our future. Childhood may be a distinct phase from adulthood but nonetheless children live in mixed communities and need to learn the responsibility that goes with citizenship as a child and as an adult; the principles are similar. We must be careful not to be too precious about 'childhood' — it is a changing and dynamic construct over time and history

Of course, no-one would want to go backwards in time to have four year olds working in coal mines, but we must remain aware that in different cultures childhood is defined differently and that the western British definition is only one of many. For instance, children in South Asian families often take responsibilities for sibling child rearing at an early age. This is expected, as children are seen as part of a family or community (usually a village) unit rather than only as individuals. In extended families, where generations of the same family live together or in close proximity everyone has their share of responsibility. South Asian children are often proud of their ability and skill in caring for younger children.

Child-centredness.

Child-centred education and care has been part of early years practice for at least a century, but the greatest impact was made by the contribution of Jean Piaget to our understanding of child psychology. Piaget's work still prevails in many of the texts on child development. His work is usually taught in a simplistic way, and many educators have a limited knowledge and understanding of his theory of learning. Some educators are only familiar with Piaget's stages of child cognitive development, and many feel that those things outside the child's direct experience in the early years should not be taught in any context. As a general rule this is nonsense.

From the ages of 0–7 years Piaget described the child as entering three significant periods (or stages) of development; the sensory motor, the pre-operational and the concrete. What is less well known is that these stages of intellectual development cannot be given precise age bands as some text books imply. As Sylva and Lunt (1982) put it:

> The exact ages at which children typically enter or leave a stage are only approximate, and Piaget tells us, for instance, that children may enter into the concrete operational period as early as five or as late as eight. (p111, 1982)

Critics of Piaget such as Peter Bryant (1974) and Margaret Donaldson (1978) have revealed flaws in Piaget's work. They illustrate how Piaget underestimated children's ability by failing to take into account the social context within which children learn. Donaldson (1992) has ventured further and her recent work pin-points the role of the emotional aspect of learning.

Some educators may be worried that teaching children about the wider community, for instance, in an area where there are no black children, would make it difficult for children to relate to as they cannot rely on direct experience of relationships with black children. We often ignore the fact that most children will have some experience of 'race' through the media and perhaps through hearing others talk about black and other ethnic minorities. This could explain why a four year old from a 'white area' who was visiting a cousin in a multi-ethnic area, refused to sit next to a black child in his cousin's nursery. Or the white three year old in a remote but exclusively white community who, on meeting a black person for the first time assumed that he was a boxer!

These are sad examples of young white children taking on negative or stereotypical views of black people because they have no opportunity in the home or care/education setting to see the way black and ethnic minority families live their lives every day. We need to give children the relevant experiences through images and activities which allow them to explore racial difference and be willing to deal with racial prejudice when it arises.

During a training session with some nursery nurses on developing an equality curriculum we began to discuss the issue of children making racist comments to other children. We established that in most cases the racism came from the home via parents or older siblings. I explained that young children should have explained to them that racism is wrong, and that as 'significant' others we should do this sensitively and not say that it is the child itself who is wrong. I was surprised to be challenged by one young woman who said; *'Oh, but that's against everything we learnt at college, it's not child-centred, because you're supposed to bring the home and the nursery together, not emphasise difference. Won't you also be saying that the child's parents are wrong?'*

This was obviously an interesting dilemma for the group. I had not anticipated that we would not have a shared set of values. However, I was

able to illustrate to the group that children could understand that different rules existed in different contexts. More importantly I was concerned with the ethical values that we held as a society, and asked the group if they would not intervene if a child were being abused physically or sexually by parents? The whole group agreed that this kind of behaviour was unacceptable by any parent; it was an abuse of power and children had a right to be free from it. We came to the conclusion that early childhood educators should discuss openly, with each other and the parents, the ethical code by which every-one should behave without devaluing others. This is an important process when developing policy on equal opportunities.

We can raise issues of 'race', culture or racism with children through stories, drama, music, art etc. and be prepared to discuss them in an open way appropriate to the age of the children. To believe that being child-centred imprisons children within their experiences would be like admitting that educators had no role to play in interacting with the children. It makes much more sense to interpret child-centredness as a process whereby we identify where the child is now, identify an educational starting point, and build upon it over time through planned activities and experiences.

Planning for and developing a relevant curriculum

Good social relationships are often fostered by planning a curriculum which provides opportunities for the children to learn more about the lives and work of the people in school and the wider community. The children's awareness of diversity in custom and culture and their respect for and understanding of cultural differences are effectively developed through planned activities and the use of carefully selected stories and picture books, artefacts and materials. (p12, DES, 1989).

This is typical of the bland multicultural statements in official documents (see also DES, 1990). They are meant to be helpful but, without first combining these statements with real exploration of the issues, educators find it difficult to implement them without clear guidance. We need to begin by developing and understanding the theoretical framework within which those who work in education and care can begin to position and develop their curriculum. This may sound daunting, but it is well worth attempting to understand because it will help those in early years settings to see how far they have progressed towards racial equality.

Four main perspectives can be identified, within or between which most of us work (three of which are adapted from Twitchin 1985). Each perspective carries a set of beliefs and therefore practices, which shape the curriculum and the children's experiences. These are as follows:

1. In the separatist (or overtly racist perspective) early childhood setting, educators are likely to hold some of the following beliefs:

   ☐ that British culture is superior because of its imperial and economic heritage and its commitment to justice, morality and Christian worship.

   ☐ that all children are the same and that sameness of treatment is sufficient regardless of colour, cultural, linguistic, religious, gender or class background;

☐ that no extra resources should be provided to 'pander' to the needs of immigrants;

☐ if immigrant parents are dissatisfied with their service they should remove their child rather than expect the service to change.

2. In the assimilationist (also referred to as the integrationist or mono-cultural perspective) early childhood setting, educators are likely to hold some of the following beliefs:

☐ that British culture is superior because most people know about our culture and the English language is spoken world-wide;

☐ that British childrearing practices are the best because they are based on Western practices and therefore this should be a universal view of childrearing;

☐ that ethnic minority or 'coloured' children would be better off if they became as much like their white English counter-parts as possible;

☐ that children whose home language is not English are disad-vantaged, and will find it difficult to learn until they can speak English;

☐ that extra resources should be made available e.g. for English language support, to integrate children as quickly as possible to the English way of life;

☐ in all-white early years settings there is 'no problem' because there are no ethnic minorities or 'coloured' people;

☐ that parents should be encouraged to speak to their children in English;

☐ that celebrating or educating children about other cultures or festivals is pointless because we are all in Britain and 'they' should learn that 'when in Rome do as the Romans do.'

3. In the multiculturalist (also referred to as the interculturalist or cultural diversity/pluralist perspective) early childhood setting, edu-cators are likely to hold some of the following beliefs:

☐ that ethnic minority children have a right to be in Britain and are an established part of our society;

☐ that ethnic minority festivals should be celebrated and all children should learn about some other cultures, religions and languages;

☐ that the cultural diversity in our society should be reflected across most areas of the curriculum;

☐ if young children are exposed to other cultures at an early stage they are unlikely to be prejudiced because most prejudice is based on ignorance of other cultures;

☐ that white parents may find it difficult to understand a multicultural curriculum therefore it should be implemented slowly. Although most parents are likely to be open-minded some may hold prejudiced views about ethnic minorities because they are misguided or belong to extremist groups;

☐ that ethnic minority parents can be made to feel welcome by putting up multilingual posters and creating a warm and welcoming atmosphere. The more 'educated', and literate ethnic minority parents should be encouraged to help out with multicultural cooking, reading bilingual stories and festival celebrations;

☐ that ethnic minorities should have a right to maintain their linguistic and cultural heritage.

4. In the anti-racist (also referred to as the racial equality perspective) early years setting, educators are likely to hold some of the following beliefs:

☐ that black and ethnic minority people have a right to be in Britain because they were invited during labour shortages in British industry;

☐ that Britain exploited and gained great material advantage from exploiting black people's countries and promoting white superiority;

☐ that all our institutions, including care and education, still reflect racist structures and procedures which systematically disadvantage black and ethnic minority parents, children and workers;

☐ only through the proactive promotion of black cultures, languages and black workers can the barriers created by racism be diminished;

☐ that most children and parents are likely to reflect the racism that is prevalent in our society and early childhood settings need clear policies and procedures for dealing with this;

☐ that all children need to learn how to talk about, and counter, unfair generalisations about ethnicity and colour;

☐ that early years settings and services should support black and ethnic minority families in their struggle against every day racism;

☐ that all staff are trained, familiar with, and capable of using, the Race Relations Act, Children Act and Education Reform Act to promote anti-racist practices, procedures and structures;

☐ that the early years educators should consciously represent the black experience, and black and ethnic minority cultures throughout the curriculum.

Most early childhood settings appear to be working towards the multicultural perspective. In areas where their are significant numbers of black and ethnic minorities some early years workers and settings have felt confident enough to take a more anti-racist and racial equality stance. The poorest models of racial equality (those settings that are segregationist or assimilationist) are still often found in largely white areas.

This remains a huge challenge to those of us who believe that children should be educated for a multi-ethnic society, rather than a mere locality. It is also a problem because, as discussed in chapters one and two, white people are still the perpetrators and perpetuators of racism. Far from the belief that anti-racist education and care is not important in white localities being true, the evidence suggests the complete opposite. The most important place to develop racial equality care and education is in largely white areas.

The curriculum should, as the Education Reform Act (1988) states, be broad and balanced. It should also provide continuity and progression and be differentiated to meet individual needs, but most of all it needs to be relevant. Relevant to the cultural backgrounds of the children and to our ethnically mixed society. The cross-curricula themes and dimensions are a useful guide for nurseries and infant schools, but could also act as a starting point for other early childhood settings.

The NCC (1992) view the dimensions within a multiculturalist perspective and assert that:

> The dimensions cover all aspects of equal opportunities and education for life in a multicultural society. Providing equal opportunities for pupils means:
>
> — treating pupils as individuals with their own abilities, difficulties, attitudes, backgrounds and experiences;
> — challenging myths, stereotypes and misconceptions;
> — ensuring that equal access to the curriculum means real opportunity to benefit:

Educating pupils for life in a multicultural society means:

> — extending pupils' knowledge and understanding of different cultures, languages and faiths;
> — valuing cultural diversity by drawing on pupils' backgrounds and experiences;
> — offering images and role models from other cultures;
> — The dimensions permeate the curriculum and are the responsibility of all teachers (p15, 1992).

Although this has become a legal requirement it is hard to envisage how teachers will prioritise this kind of work, given that it is not part of the assessed curriculum. It is left to schools and their governing bodies to implement as they see fit. The five cross-curricular themes are also of value in planning for a balanced and relevant curriculum:

1. *Economical and industrial understanding*, e.g. during a topic on shopping.
2. *Careers education and guidance*, e.g. during a topic on 'people who help us'.
3. *Health education*, e.g. during work on 'the body' or 'food'.

4. *Education for citizenship*, e.g. during work which emphasises caring, sharing and responsibility, for instance taking care of another child or setting the tables for lunch.
5. *Environment education*, e.g. during a topic on 'mini-beasts',' the weather' or 'our local area'.

Each of these themes, as well as the Foundation Subjects of the national curriculum provides the basis for anti-racist curriculum (Runnymede Trust, 1993). When educators are planning their curriculum for young children it is often helpful to start by cross-checking what has been planned with a checklist devised by the staff of the key features of education and care for racial equality.

A curriculum which is anti-racist may exhibit some of the following features. It will

☐ develop an understanding that people come from a range of backgrounds and cultures and offer children a secure environment in which to explore their own culture;

☐ offer opportunities for children to explore that no culture, language or religion is more superior than others;

☐ depict a range of families (see *What is a Family?* by Braun and Eisenstadt, 1990, Development Education Centre);

☐ show people from a range of ethnic backgrounds doing everyday things e.g. in the park, at meal time, on a family outing or shopping;

☐ use the children's interests in planning, and to extend their learning;

☐ find appropriate resources and examples from a range of cultures for each topic over and above the everyday multicultural toys, posters etc;

☐ depict a range of child rearing practices from different cultures;

☐ help children to talk about and challenge stereotypes;

☐ promote social and emotional development, and teach about caring and sharing;

☐ involve parents and community groups in visiting and talking/working with the children;

☐   illustrate through the curriculum that human achievements are universal and not just western;

☐   expect high standards of achievement from all the children.

It would be much more helpful to each early childhood setting to devise a checklist for its own centre, to take account of the ages of the children, the resources available and the past experience of anti-racist curriculum.

The importance of concrete experiences and play

Anyone who has worked with young children and observed how they learn from the world around them cannot help being struck by the main medium through which they choose to learn, play. As Margaret Lally puts it:

> For young children, who have considerably less knowledge and understanding of the world than adults, and for whom so much knowledge is new and exciting and so many physical skills still have to be acquired, the need for exploration and experimentation is even more important (p72, 1991).

As Moyles (1989), Hurst (1991) and most early years workers would argue, Lally (1991) goes on to say that children need a variety of play materials which can act as a vehicle for the young child's learning, because play is a natural motivator for the child. She asserts that play offers children the chance to explore and discover, to construct a range of materials, to repeat and consolidate skills, to represent, create, imagine and to develop their social and emotional worlds.

We also know that children need to build on their prior knowledge and understandings of the world through making sense of old experiences and facing new ones. The educators' task is to provide appropriate concrete materials to aid this development. All children, but especially children whose home language is not English, will require materials which will stimulate the senses. Things that can be tasted, manipulated, smelled, seen and heard are able to provide the first hand experiences the young child needs.

These experiences allow children to articulate and describe what they comprehend and to link the meanings of words to their cognitive understanding. Without the experience of dramatic and imaginative play through puppets, other toys and materials it is difficult for educators to respond to the children's ideas. Adults should get involved in play with children and where appropriate help them to extend their language and conceptual understanding. However, children also enjoy solitary play and the educator must judge carefully when intervention is appropriate, whether it be a single question or more extended involvement.

The meanings we derive from our experiences, past and present, need to be framed in language. For young children language acquisition, whether first or second language, is of major importance to their day to day and future success.

Social integration and small group work

The children and adults in an early childhood setting are a key resource to child development, and particularly to social and co-operative development. Children can work and play together to share ideas, tackle problems together, and serve as role models for a culturally diverse community. For the educators in a particular setting, grouping should be given careful consideration. If children learn a great deal from each other they need to experience being with different children in different contexts.

The educator needs to manage her time appropriately so as to give each child some attention, according to individual needs. She needs to make sure that the time she has is well structured and in this context group work can be very beneficial to the children and at the same time allow the educator to work with more than one child.

There are three main advantages to small group work. Children get the chance to talk and listen in a small and safe context and are encouraged to speak. It allows the educator to make close observations and to record the child's learning. It also frees the educator to focus on a small group, to interact and to extend each child's learning. This can be done during outdoor play too. Adults can get involved with small groups of two to four children in house or sand play, or through a game initiated by the adult.

In a mixed ability, mixed language and culture early years setting the educator should consider a variety of group organisational strategies. Groups can be based on friendships for activities such as music, drama and home corner play. For some activities other criteria for grouping can be used, for instance, if a story is to be told entirely in a home language by a parent it would be acceptable to have a group of same home language children (although no child should be refused admission to a group).

Children who spend some time in an ethnically or linguistically homogeneous group should also have the opportunity to listen to stories in mixed language groups. If there are bilingual educators working with the children they should work with ethnically mixed groups but should try to support the bilingual children's learning using English and the home language.

Stories, books and language awareness

Book areas and libraries deserve special mention because of the powerful way in which they illustrate and represent the world for children. Children need to be exposed to a variety of books. Of course favourite stories which the children enjoy having read to them over and over again (even if the adults are fed up with hearing them repeatedly!) are a must for any collection. Alongside these there should be a range of books: story books, dual language books, folk stories, poetry books, information and reference books, books made by the children and books about children in other countries with storylines familiar to children's experiences the world over.

Books are also responsible for shaping children's understanding about different ethnic groups. Exposing children to a variety of literature can help them to understand the similarities and differences between different religions, cultures and languages. Most importantly, books allow issues to be raised and false notions can be challenged sensitively. However, we must remember (as we saw in Chapter one) that children are normally socialised in a racist and sexist context and will quite often challenge anything they perceive to differ from the social norms.

For instance, I remember telling a group of young children the story of *Emily the Engine Driver* written by Charles and Juliet Snape. They enjoyed the story because Emily is crazy about engines and engines appear in all the illustrations and the children love to point them out and talk about them. The story ends on Emily's birthday when she gets to drive an engine during her birthday outing to a fair. I asked the children if they thought Emily would become an engine driver when she grew up and some were adamant that she would not. They gave a number of reasons, such as, 'The lever will be too heavy for her to lift'; 'She can't because she's a girl'; 'Because her brains jumbled up!'. The boy who made this last statement explained that this was because she was a girl.

The strength of feeling with which the children, both boys and girls, made these statements, made the staff plan a great deal more carefully for permeating the curriculum with anti-sexism. The way the 'Emily' incident ended was pertinent: during the discussion one girl said that her aunt was an engine driver. When it was learnt that her aunt lived in Scotland, the boy showing the greatest resistance to the concept of a female engine driver retorted: 'Well, things must be up-side-down in Scotland!'. Even in the face of evidence children can resist changing their attitudes, which only emphasises the importance that all our work be framed in an equality ethos.

In relation to books for racial equality Clark and Millikan (1986) state that:

> Young children are vulnerable to stereotypes and bias in books as at this stage they are forming perceptions of themselves and others. Literature should focus on similarities of groups, rather than presenting stories which only draw attention to exotic differences (p8, 1986).

This is true but adults need to know how to handle the materials and also the children's enquiries and prejudices as they arise, while also making long term plans for dealing with the issues across the curriculum.

The issue of using checklists to select against choosing racist books is one that worries some people. This should not be a problem if we accept that racism is wrong, in the same way that many educators would not choose a book if it were inaccurate or if it was offensive to their own ethnic background. Staff may want to create their own checklist to select information and story books, along the lines of the following which are adapted from Bakar et al. (1991) and Hazareesingh et al. (1989):

☐ How well does the story line relate to the children's home backgrounds?

☐ Are the black and ethnic minority characters always associated with poverty and 'primitive' living conditions?

☐ Are the illustrations clear, colourful and large enough to make the story easy to follow?

☐ Is the language appropriately simple, and does it allow repetition of words?

☐ Does the book/story encourage the children to participate actively? e.g. the open-and-close illustrations in Rod Campbell's book, *Dear Zoo*, invites children to take an active interest.

☐ Does the book allow the children to gain insights into other people's emotions, cultures and experiences?

☐ Do the white characters always hold the power and make the most important decisions?

☐ Are the black characters in the book shown as stupid, disruptive, menacing or subservient to others in the text?

☐ Does the way a story is written and described help children to value each other and the cultural backgrounds in the setting and beyond?

☐ Are the illustrations of black people life-like or do they look like white people painted black or illustrated in a caricatured way?

If staff are unhappy about a book it is not enough simply to remove it. It is worth writing to the publisher to explain why the book is unacceptable. Language awareness is an important aspect to develop for all early years settings but it is vital in the mainly monolingual setting. To develop a positive attitude to each child's whole linguistic resource means more than appreciating ethnic minority languages. The variety within any single language — and English is no exception — can be used creatively. We need to devise activities that allow children to explore notions of accent, dialect and register. A good starting point is to look at the way children and staff use or say particular words and then raise the issue through a game. This encourages children to listen, talk and conjecture about why people talk differently.

The educator is always there to help the children formulate their explanations. Another valuable activity is to elicit from the children how many different ways they know for naming something: for instance, the word dog can get children thinking about their, or a sibling's use of 'baby language', so doggie, bow-wow and woof-woof may be mentioned. In a multilingual setting the educator can say the word in Urdu, Panjabi or whichever language is spoken by the children, as well as in French or a language the educator knows other than English. In a setting where children feel comfortable and secure they will volunteer words in their home language, but children should not be forced to say things in their first language if they do not want to.

Children should be encouraged to speak in their home language to each other and during role-play. Keeping an old telephone in the setting, for children to pretend to ring up parents and friends often encourages conversations/talk in the home language. Dual language books and tapes, both commercial and those made by children and parents (involving parents helps a great deal) should be freely available. Labels and multi-lingual posters, (although associated with 'tokenism' — because that is all some settings do!) are valuable as part of a wider language awareness strategy, giving the children and community the message that the setting values diversity. Staff should learn and use a range of words, rhymes and songs that can be enjoyed by all.

Posters, puzzles and toys

The Working Group Against Racism in Children's Resources (1990) have produced a useful guide for the evaluation and selection of toys and other resources for children. This is helpful because most educators are not aware of the powerful stereotypes that are promoted through some toys. Many educational suppliers have woken up to the fact that early years educators want manipulative toys which reflect our multi-ethnic society. The same suppliers are also producing more sophisticated and better puzzles and posters.

Each setting should have a resource bank of toys, posters, puzzles, maps and labelled photographs which reflect positive images of black people and help the children see that their whole world is diverse and that this is the norm.

The 'homecorner'

This is a changing area of the early childhood setting, becoming a cafe or a hospital or even a shop. It is not practical to explore how each of these conversions could be made anti-racist but we can highlight what could go into a 'homecorner' or play area. Each child can convert the 'homecorner' into his or her own space, reflecting the things that they know about and the people and experiences in their lives outside the early years setting. A great deal of co-operative play occurs as children act out other characters and alternative roles and fictitious events. Some educators do not like the term 'homecorner' regarding it as gendered and conducive to gender stereotyping so this may require discussion in your setting.

Some careful thinking and resourcing can make the 'homecorner' into a wonderful educational arena. In order to promote anti-racist values children need to be surrounded by the beauty from a variety of cultural contexts and everyday artefacts which encourage and promote cultural diversity and challenge stereotypes. Some of the following ideas may be helpful. Try and add to this list if you are working with young children, brainstorming ideas with your colleagues.

☐ Decorate the homecorner with photo albums showing families from a variety of ethnic backgrounds and posters that portray festivals and other cultural events. Beautifully decorative material bought from African-Caribbean, South American or South Asian shops and market stalls can be hung on walls, cover small tables or cushions. Birthday and greeting cards depicting black people should be displayed appropriate to the event. There should be mirrors (in plastic frames) so that the children can look at themselves. Small rugs for the floor can add warmth and make the area cosy.

☐ Kitchen utensils from a range of cultures can now be purchased from educational suppliers but can be costly. It is worth supplementing your collection by visiting local towns where there are black and ethnic minority communities and buying utensils from local shops. There are real bargains and it can be great fun. You can buy such things as small rolling pins, boards and a 'thava' (flat pan) for chappati making, and small stainless steel or plastic thali bowls and trays. There are tea-sets, pans, Chinese woks, small bowls, chopsticks, pasta servers and empty boxes and packets of food. Some sealed, 'child-proof' clear plastic containers with a range of pulses such as black-eye beans, lentils and split peas and items might arouse curiosity or link with the home, for instance, mustard seeds, pasta shapes and whole spices.

☐ Dressing-up clothes are a favourite with some children and any collection should contain a range of everyday clothes for both sexes from a variety of backgrounds and ages. National costumes are not very useful as they are unlikely to provide a realistic impression of a culture. Small items such as scarves and jewellery made from a range of materials can contribute to a stimulating collection.

☐ Dolls are important to children. A range of authentic looking black dolls depicting different ages and ethnic groups should be available to children alongside white dolls. Some educational suppliers also sell doll heads with different types of hair such as African hair which can be braided. Dressing-up clothes for dolls should be available.

☐ Food made from play-dough, quite often made by children for when the 'homecorner' becomes a cafe should remain in the area. These could include pizzas, eggs, samosas, spring rolls, bread, chappattis and fruit and vegetables which have been made and painted by the children.

☐ Items that enhance talk and communication such as a telephone, pads for 'writing' shopping lists, menus, books and a cut-out television screen made of cardboard, initiate a great deal of co-operative and communicative play.

The 'homecorner' should be a changing and stimulating area for play and one which reflects our multi-ethnic society.

Festivals

We can learn about festivals and give young children a range of experiences which help them to understand the importance of festivals to all people. Obviously it is impossible, and undesirable to try to cover all the festivals or even most of them. Many early childhood educators are anxious to 'celebrate' festivals, but it is surely more important to 'educate' about festivals and this can be done through a variety of activities. Some of the festivals that can be celebrated are Chinese New Year (Yuan Tan), Chinese Moon Festival; Hindu festivals of Holi and Diwali; Muslim festivals of Eid ul-Fitr and Eid ul-Adha; Sikh festivals of Diwali and Guru Nanak's birthday; Jewish festivals of Rosh Hashana and Hannukah and Christian festivals of Christmas and Easter.

Each of these festivals is suitable for young children to learn about through drama, live theatre, stories and through cooking special foods and making greeting cards. There are also, however, festivals which are unsuitable for young children to try to understand. For staff at early years settings the first priority should be to acquire a good festival calendar and some books on the various faiths. If the setting is in a multi-ethnic area parents can contribute a good deal. Photographs of families preparing for and celebrating a festival can be made into superb books. Parents can advise on customs, respect, sequence of events, the story behind the festival and how to dress, make an appropriate card or cook special foods.

Snack times and cooking

These are important routine and educational experiences in all early childhood settings. Food generally — in its preparation, where it comes from and the routine of mealtimes in families — makes it a universal experience. The educational experiences derived from the preparation, cooking and sharing of food enables children to learn about health, safety, hygiene, measuring, science, nutrition and develops their vocabulary and language generally.

Cooking and sharing food is a very enjoyable and social activity which allows for a great deal of practical work, and stimulates talk related to the senses of feeling, smelling, tasting and seeing food change during the cooking process. This is very good for bilingual learners, who require practically related language to increase their vocabulary and to make sense of the processes of activity, terms such as: mixing, stirring, slicing, cutting, heating, dissolving and so on. In addition to acquiring terms and skills, children are learning to work in groups and share a task.

Educators should make every attempt to offer a diverse range of cooking experiences. Not all the 'exotic' cooking should be done by the black and ethnic minority staff or parents. There is no reason why the white educators should not cook pizzas, chappattis, black-eyed beans and rice or South Asian sweets with the children. Similarly, black and ethnic-minority parents and educators could make bread, soup, fruit salad or gingerbread biscuits with the children.

Educators will need to be sensitive and informed about cultural and religious taboos associated with certain foods for different ethnic minority groups and individual restrictions for social or medical reasons. For instance, parents who are vegetarians by religious belief or because of animal rights commitments or for health reasons need to have their children's dietary habits respected. When children begin at the setting, parents should be asked about the child's food requirements, and religious taboos should be respected. For example, the Jewish and Muslim religions forbid the eating of any pig meat or pig product, so pork, lard, bacon, pork sausages etc. must not be given to children from these faiths.

Music, rhymes and songs

Children love to listen and move to music and actively to participate in familiar songs and rhymes. A variety of cassette recordings of music from around the world and different styles of music should be collected, to be played during movement and dance activities, or for listening to in the 'homecorner'. Children should have opportunities to hear a range of music, but also to see it being played. Ideally there should be a collection of musical instruments for the children to play with and for educators to use in playing rhythmic games.

Children can be taught finger rhymes (finger puppets are a source of delight for most children) and songs in community languages. Efforts should also be made to introduce children to rhymes and songs in European languages. Educational suppliers and bookshops now sell song and assembly books which are multicultural in content. Musical instruments like tablas (Indian drums), maracas and castanets (South American), pipes, recorders and cymbals (from various countries) can all add to the enjoyment of music appreciation and understanding of rhythm. Parents may be willing to talk about any instruments they have at home or come in and play for the children or teach them songs and rhymes. Educators should take the opportunity to develop their own book of children's favourite songs, in transliteration if necessary.

Values and behaviour

This chapter started with the question: What is education for? Most people would agree that we educate and care for our children because we want them to become active learners, with a positive self-image and the capacity to become independent thinkers. We want our children to be able to communicate effectively with others and hold the fundamental values of caring and sharing, even within a society geared towards competition. The formative years of a child's development is where the foundations for these skills, attitudes, knowledge and concepts are laid.

Early childhood educators have an instrumental role to play in this development. Anne Stonehouse (1991) defines discipline as: 'helping children learn to guide their own behaviour in a way that shows respect and caring for themselves, other people, and the physical environment' (p77, 1991). Clearly, then, values education goes hand-in-hand with discipline and behaviour management.

The way that adults and children relate to each other in any setting is an indication of the ethos of that setting. To create a positive ethos for racial equality every setting will need to explore: what the ethos in their setting feels like to the users e.g. parents, children and workers; what behaviours, procedures and structures create the ethos; what aspects of the existing provision is positive and what negative; and who is responsible for change.

Children need help from the adults around them in learning how to care for each other and to share things. To help the children in this respect, the educator must have the children's trust. Young children's capacity to reflect and see things from another person's point of view is not fully developed. Most small children find it difficult to see another person's view as equally important. Consideration for others has to be learnt. According to Stonehouse, children need educators who will consciously be:

— encouraging positive interactions;

— calling attention to other points of view;

— encouraging communication with others;

— trying to ensure that they learn constructive ways to resolve differences;

— promoting co-operation, not competition. (p78, 1991)

Of course educators cannot expect children to behave in this way if they do not practice the same behaviour themselves. If children see us showing kindness, patience, love, empathy, respect and care for others they are more likely to want to emulate such behaviour. Conflict resolution is an important aspect of learning to live with others. Louise Dermon Sparks (1989) asserts that:

> For children to feel good and confident about themselves they need to be able to say 'That's not fair,' or 'I don't like that,' if they are the target of prejudice and discrimination. For children to develop empathy and respect for diversity, they need to be able to say, 'I don't like what you are doing' to a child who is abusing another child. If we teach children to recognise justice, then we must also teach them that people can create positive change by working together. (p77, 1989).

For many educators the experience of working actively with children in this way may be underdeveloped, especially when it comes to dealing with racism and racist incidents. This is because traditionally educators have not been trained for this and because their knowledge base on issues of racism is poor. So it is not surprising that when overt racism does occur it is often ignored or dealt with inappropriately. Each setting, as part of their 'race' equality policy will need to discuss the issue of racist harassment and devise procedures for dealing with it. In chapter two we learned that racism is normalised in our society, which means that parents, children and educators are likely to need help in acquiring a positive perception of black and ethnic minority groups.

We can take some of the following actions in dealing with incidents of a racist nature, in particular when children are involved in racist name-calling:

☐ **Short term action**

— if you hear a racist remark do not ignore it or you will be condoning the behaviour and therefore complying with the remarks;

— state your position immediately by condemning the remarks as unacceptable behaviour in the setting. As a 'significant' other in the child's life, s/he is likely to learn from your value position;

— explain clearly why the remarks made were wrong and hurtful or offensive, and ask the abused child how s/he felt so that both children can begin to think actively about the incident;

— do not attack the child who has been racist in a personal manner or imply that the child as a person is wrong, only that what was said is wrong;

— explain in appropriate terms to the abuser why the comment was wrong, and give both children the correct information;

— support and physically comfort the abused child, making sure that she knows that you support her identity and that of her community group and spend some time working with her on the activity she is engaged with;

— at some point during the same day, work with the child who made the racist remarks to ensure that she knows that you continue to value her as a person.

☐ **Long term action**

— target the parents of children who make racist comments to ensure that they understand your policy for racial equality, and that you will not accept abuse against any child. Point out how this damages their child;

— develop topics and read stories which raise issues of racial similarities and differences and encourage the children to talk about their understandings and feelings;

— create the kind of ethos that promotes and values black and ethnic minority images and contributions to society;

— involve parents and children (depending on the age of the children) in decision making processes, particularly during the development of a policy on equality;

— talk through your equality policy with all parents as and when children enter the setting, along with the other information parents need.

— develop appropriate teaching and learning strategies for children who are acquiring English so that they do not get bored, frustrated and tempted to be naughty — negative labelling is a common problem.

Child profiles and assessment

Observing children, making assessments about their progress and future learning, and recording this information in individual child profiles is at the heart of well-planned and effective learning for the early years. Many early years specialists have written about the value and processes of assessment (see Lally, 1991; Hurst, 1991; Sylva et al., 1980; Sylva et al., 1990 and Drummond and Rouse, 1992) but few have made any specific reference to black or ethnic minority pupils and assessment. Consequently there is very little guidance to be found on recording and assessment of children who have English as a second language. A notable exception is the Inner London Primary Language Record, which explicitly records the progress of bilingual children. However it does not deal with the youngest children.

Observation is obviously one of the best ways to understand and learn about a child's development and learning progress. In recording our observations of individual children over time, we can build up a picture of a child's learning needs, and this can help us to plan an appropriate curriculum. Educators can also evaluate the provision they make for different aspects of the curriculum and remedy any problems where necessary.

Our observations of the children also provide a forum for discussion with others within the team we work in, or with the colleagues a child is to go on to. Observations do not always have to be systematically recorded on schedules. We can observe children at any time and make a quick mental or written note of what we have seen or heard. This can happen during outdoor play, storytime or at the activity table.

The important thing is to make records and to use them regularly to inform practice. What information should a profile contain? A profile should provide us with an all round picture of a child's development in the setting. When children begin nursery, playgroup or going to a child-minder it is natural to ask the parents for information about their child. This first encounter with the parent is critical because of the first impressions for both parties. What parents can tell you about their child is where the profile should begin, and the following are some areas which should be recorded. If the parents do not speak English very well do this through an interpreter. Make sure that you do not rush the parent — if there is a policy of home visiting the following information may be collected more usefully in the parent/carers home:

☐ details of the child's early development as a baby or toddler, including any medical or social conditions or emotionally stressful periods;

☐ personal details about the child as an individual: likes and dislikes, food preferences, toilet training etc.;

☐ details of cultural and religious background, for instance, making sure you know how to pronounce the child's name correctly, knowing the cultural or religious factors affecting dietary requirements and dress. Do ask the parents what names are given to particular items of clothing if you do not already know e.g. shalwar and kameez are the names for the dress and trouser worn by South Asian females;

☐ details about the family: who has looked after the child, who can be expected to pick her up after sessions in the setting, number of younger and older siblings;

☐ language competence in English and any other home languages: examples of what the child can say, who she talks to, how much television is watched, which stories is she familiar with and what experience she has of books in English and home language. Note all the home languages;

☐ social and emotional development including how the child gets on with other children, any problems such as bed wetting, anxieties or special loves of particular objects, people, games, songs or toys;

☐ details about the child's physical development: both small and gross motor development, opportunities to draw, paint, play out side or swim etc.;

☐ any other details the parents would like to give.

This would be the starting point. During the discussions with parents it should be made clear that the profile is ongoing, and that the parents' views on the child's progress or any report on changes in circumstances is always welcome. Invite parents to view the profile regularly and comment on it.

Regular observations should allow educators to add more headings to the profile, to monitor children's development in areas such as: science and technology, language/s, humanities, art and craft. Also factual information about attendance, self-reliance, relationships with adults and peers and self-esteem and identity.

In providing a curriculum for racial equality it is important to remember that assessments should be checked for stereotypical assumptions and that the provision we make for learning is free from discrimination. Our knowledge is not value-free, therefore our assessments need to be monitored. The best way to achieve this is to talk to other staff and consciously to evaluate the statements that we make regarding each child's progress.

For children who are learning English as a second language the monitoring of their learning more generally and, in particular, cognitive learning is critical. Far too many educators unintentionally delay challenging second language learners cognitively until the children have mastered enough English. This is denying children access to the curriculum, and strategies must be employed to move beyond this stage.

CHAPTER 5

Parental involvement: fostering confidence and communication

In recent years we have been led to believe that the government is increasingly concerned to foster parental choice and participation in the process of their children's education. This concern has largely been manifested through the Education Reform Act (1988) which only applies to the school sector. Parents have, in line with market philosophy, more 'choice' in selecting the school that their child attends and a right to regular reports on academic achievement. In response to a perceived failure of schools to inform and involve parents, the government has issued a parents' charter outlining the rights that parents have been given.

In the early years sector there has been a longer, more established and more sophisticated history of parental involvement which goes beyond mere 'choice'. Of course it is also important that parents can choose from a range of early childhood services and that they are kept informed of their child's development. But what most early years settings have been striving for is a real partnership between parents and educators, and increased involvement in the early years setting (see Pugh and De'Ath, 1984; Pugh et al., 1987). However most of the current literature on the subject of parents fails to deal with racism or the specific issues surrounding black parental involvement.

Gillian Klein (1993) argues that black and ethnic minority families have become more actively involved in their children's education. Some second and third generation black communities have become increasingly aware of the positive role models provided by the achievements of black members of parliament, television personalities, authors and teachers. Klein goes on to say:

It is less common among this generation of ethnic minority parents, many British-born themselves and mistrustful of the education system as a result of their own experiences, simply to hand over their children to the care of schools as the immigrant generation had so trustingly done. Ethnic minority families discuss the issues of racism much more openly, both among themselves and in the wider society, and are more watchful of all public service provision, and more informed of their rights (p9, 1993).

While undoubtedly true for some, other black and ethnic minority parents and families continue to find it difficult to cope with their own circumstances let alone to feel they can enter the early childhood setting and become 'involved' in their children's formal education. Of course this is true of both ethnic minority and ethnic majority families when economic survival becomes the first day-to-day priority. The experience of racism and discrimination in employment in particular, makes such priorities even more common among black working class families. In these circumstances educators have to think through careful strategies for accepting, supporting and encouraging parents. Until parents can trust the educators there is little point in expecting their active support. Julia Gilkes (1989) in her book, *Developing Nursery Education* provides a moving chapter on how one nursery centre worked towards gaining the trust of families in a white, working-class community in Kirkby.

In the chapter Gilkes explains how parents were encouraged to get involved in the nursery. In some cases this meant educators first supporting the parents and their children in many ways and for several years before the parents felt ready to come forward. Parents had first to feel supported, helped and valued before they could reciprocate by participating in a partnership sense. This principle probably applies to most settings:

parents first and foremost need to feel that the setting offers them something, such as friendship, advice, support or even just a chance to have coffee and meet other parents and carers. What Gilkes (1989) is really saying is that centres have to get their ethos right. A supportive, even therapeutic, setting that creates confidence in those who come. An atmosphere or ethos that encourages a sense of belonging should aim to:

☐ make everyone feel that they are wanted and that they have a positive role to play in the setting;

☐ show parents that they can always make their feelings, views and opinions known to the staff, and that these will be dealt with respectfully and seriously;

☐ demonstrate that the parents' linguistic, cultural and religious backgrounds are valued and seen as positive assets to the setting;

☐ show that the early years setting is an organic part of the community it serves and so understands the concerns, aspirations and difficulties the members of that community might face.

The Children Act (Volume 2, 1989) states that parents of young children have certain parental rights which allow them to influence the quality of care their child receives. They should be able to acquire information about the setting, choose between settings, and modify, express views about and contribute to their child's setting. This has serious implications for parents who are not confident about their English. Early childhood educators need to ensure that they offer the whole community an equal chance to understand and use their service. If this means translating notices about the setting and putting them in areas where ethnic minority families will see them, e.g. doctors' surgeries, then this should be done as a first step to ensure initial interest.

Parents' preconceived views on education

Not all parents whose children attend our early years settings will have had a positive experience of education themselves, and because most of us draw on our past experiences to make judgements about matters of everyday life, parents might well hold negative views about educators and the institutions they represent. They might even be sceptical or suspicious of professionals in general, particularly in areas where parents perceive professionals as dominating and controlling their lives. Parents who are unemployed, who live in rented accommodation or suffer regular interventions in their family life by social workers and other support agencies, may feel powerless and that they have little control over their lives or making decisions.

This cumulative past experience and sense of outside control can make some parents feel disempowered and lacking in confidence in their dealings with early years workers. Their own academic failure may be attributed directly to schooling or their perception that they personally were, and perhaps still are, not capable people. In the past, schools might have led them to believe that they were lacking in ability and potential. Years of undermined self-confidence and inner articulation of themselves as being incapable could make some parents doubtful about their ability to be good educators to their own children, let alone to get actively involved in their child's education through nurseries, playgroup, school and so forth.

Educators, then, clearly need to take some responsibility for building confidence and for getting to know parents as people with a life history which affects their everyday actions. Some parents will certainly be confident and will have had positive experiences of education, but it cannot be assumed. Most educators have had relatively positive experiences of school and education themselves, or have at least worked out the value of learning and are committed to promoting it in the lives of others. But this does not mean that we always understand or are sympathetic to the values others bring with them, shaped by their previous experiences and understandings.

Parents have culturally conceived ideas about the role of education and educators and these are likely to be somewhat different. In some cultures the role of the educators is seen as distinct and separate to the role of parenting, and educators may need to take some time explaining and illustrating how the child can benefit from partnership and continuity of educational experience across early years setting and home. It is sensible for educators not to make assumptions about parents' knowledge, beliefs or experiences but to create a friendly atmosphere where parents can talk openly about their feelings. Additionally, sufficient interest should be taken in each parent as an individual and their views and feelings should be sought on general matters pertaining to the setting and particularly to their child. This sort of interest and care fosters trust and an open and secure ambience.

Power, participation and access

For parents to participate in the daily life of an early years setting there must be real and obvious commitment from staff. It is not enough to use the rhetoric of parents as 'partners' in the education of their children. Some educators do use such phrases, and through using these words feel committed to them. In reality this is not always the case, and it is all too easy to neglect the most vulnerable and needy parents. Regular scrutiny of the slogans and rhetoric we use is essential. For instance, what do we actually mean by a 'partnership' with parents? According to Pugh and De'Ath (1989) partnership means: '..a working relationship that is characterised by a shared sense of purpose, mutual respect and the willingness to negotiate. This implies a sharing of information, responsibility, skills, decision-making and accountability' (p.33).

This is a tall order and requires a great deal of effort on the part of staff, not only in terms of the availability and usage of their service, but also of how to reach all sectors of the communities served. For example, Pugh (1988) showed through a survey of local authority practice on guide/handbooks for parents on services for under-fives, that practices varied enormously. Some authorities had produced information in ethnic minority languages, but it became clear on closer inspection that the information about services was not always reaching those who needed it (Pugh, 1988, pp62-63). So the role of individual settings in providing information locally is absolutely vital.

In the process of providing information and establishing a partnership it is staff who must take the lead responsibility — they are the ones with the power. It may not feel that way to individual staff, particularly those who have less paper qualifications or part-time contracts, but to the parents they represent the establishment, with the 'voice' that counts. All staff can work towards partnership by creating an ethos of belonging to the early years setting. This ethos should be characterised by:

☐ regular and effective communication;

☐ willingness to share information with parents about their child and the setting;

☐ willingness to ask parents for advice about their child and to seek their views on key issues such as curriculum, child rearing and assessment;

☐ working towards common goals, taking time to explain and listen carefully;

☐ visibly displaying a liking for parents and respect for their feelings;

☐ being approachable and open to negotiation;

☐ sharing responsibility and a willingness to work together;

☐ illustrating that the child is at the heart of the care and education service provided and therefore that the care/family unit is all-important.

A booklet or parent guide in the appropriate community languages can make these points clearly and succinctly. But there is no substitute for a warm and caring reception from staff at the setting. For parents who are very busy, and particularly black and ethnic minority parents some of whom may be illiterate in English and in their own language, the only medium for understanding the setting may be the personal contact. This certainly applies to only some, and not most, parents — but these are the parents that educators should particularly be communicating with.

An open and informal ethos of partnership can be fostered through willingness to share basic information. The staff can display photographs with the names of all the workers in their setting; they can inform parents of staff who are leaving and give information on new staff. Some of the day's activities could be displayed for the parents at the start of each day. Significant events of the day could be displayed when parents come to pick up their children. And in those few minutes when parents are hanging around waiting for children or staff, staff can easily supplement the regular personal contact with casual exchanges — but this is no substitute for the regular contact.

Parents' first impressions are critical and the environment they come into will tell them a good deal about the values held by the setting. A bright, lively environment with displays of children's work, multicultural and multilingual material and information for parents on local activities,

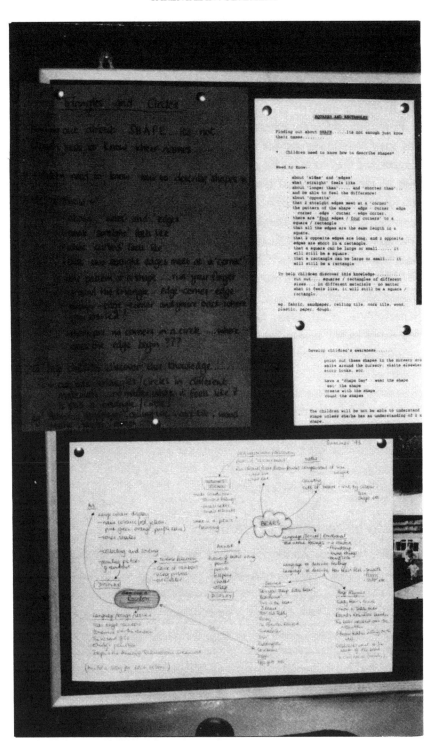

events and support groups can make for a comforting and secure impression. It is also essential always to have somebody around who can make time to listen to parents and not rush off. Parents do not always want to talk to staff — they may just want time out to have a coffee and meet and talk to other parents or use the toy library with their toddlers. Providing spaces for parents and their babies and toddlers is a valuable and very welcoming service. Parents are individuals, in specific circumstances and they have varied needs. This is true also of the service, which may be restricted in what it can provide, depending upon whether it is a school, a nursery centre or a combined facility. Expertise of staff will vary considerably as will the material resources available. It is up to individual settings to optimise their facilities and expertise to provide the best service possible and parents should be treated as top priority.

Most settings have parents on their governing bodies or management committees and their views will be important in evaluating parental participation. More often than not, these parents are seen as representatives of the whole parent body but this cannot be so. Settings in multiracial areas often have no black or ethnic minority representation. It is almost impossible to represent every parent's views but that is no reason to avoid consultation with as many parents as possible. Educators have to find ways of communicating with the full range of parents to get a better balance of perceived parental needs across class, gender, 'race' and disability within the community. Where the local community appears to be homogeneous (although this is very doubtful) efforts still need to be made to represent the wider community.

The changing needs of families.

Schools, more than nurseries, playgroups or childminders, gear their service more towards meeting the individual needs of the child, particularly in terms of cognitive development, and the national curriculum has encouraged this trend. As early years educators, our understanding of the early years of a child's life is characterised by a commitment to the child within the family as well as to the child as an individual. Most settings provide for the child as a member of a family unit and recognise the critical role played by the family in the child's early socialisation and development. Supporting and working with families is seen as a vital part of the child's development and well-being.

The nature of the family has changed dramatically over the last two decades or so, yet many training manuals and books on early childhood care pay little attention to its importance in the lives of children (Development Education Centre,1990). The perceived ' normal family' of two parents and two point two children is invalid, yet educators might still measure families against this 'norm'.

The reality is that there is no longer a 'norm', at least not the kind of 'norm' that was promoted in many of our reading schemes in schools for example. Many of us grew up reading stories and believing that a normal family has a mother, father and children. One could take this further and argue that the British societal 'norm' of a family was (and still is?) a white, married mother and father with two white offspring, genetically belonging to their parents, the boy child preferably older than the girl child. We learned that the father is the main breadwinner, working in an office while mother is confined to the home, child care and housework, that the boy is active, the girl passive. Although this may have been true for a few families and the scenario in reading schemes it is not the reality for the vast majority of family units today.

The main problem with promoting or advocating such an unrealistic model of the family as the norm is that it allows all family units different from it to be seen as (by definition) abnormal or 'deviant'. Hence we are in danger of pathologising the majority of families! Many educators are concerned lest the use of the term 'the family', conjure up such stereotypical images. There can be no clear-cut definition of the family. What we can work towards, without preconceived assumptions, is a better understanding of who cares for a child and what relationship that person or persons has to the child, so that we can work together effectively to the mutual benefit of the child and her carer/s.

Black ethnic minorities make up just over six per cent of our population. A growing number of parents are unmarried, divorced, gay, lesbian, disabled, unemployed and so forth. Some children have many brothers and sisters while others have none; some are adopted, fostered, living in children's homes or are homeless. Do any of these variations make the children or their carers/families any less deserving of a positive and caring early years service? But unless we tackle the stereotypes that some of us have come to accept we risk providing prejudiced treatment to some children and their carers, and valuing some members of our community less than others. That families are all different is quite normal. Through acknowledging these differences educators can begin to meet the needs of families.

Helping parents to deal with their own racism

It is vital that parents do not feel that you disapprove of them because they have a different culture, clothes, religion or are disabled or a single parent. This is not to say that there cannot ever be any disagreement. Parents too can hold negative and stereotyped views. For instance, what if a white parent complains because her child is mixing with ethnic minority children or playing with black dolls and she does not want her child to think that interracial relationships are normal? Or if a parent does not want her child to associate with a child whose parents are lesbians? Such situations are difficult to deal with. Educators need first to look at their own values and require training on how to handle issues of this kind and keep the respect of the parents concerned.

Educators have to be sure of the principles and educational values which determine the ethos of their setting. The United Nations Convention on the Rights of the Child is an excellent guide to good practice. It states that our aim should be to prepare:

> the child for responsible life in a free society, in the spirit of understanding, peace, tolerance, equality of sexes, and friendship among all peoples, ethnic, national and religious groups and persons of indigenous origin (1989, Article 29.1d).

These same and consistent responsibilities must apply to our daily negotiations with parents. Most parents would already be familiar with the setting's guiding educational principles and values because they will have read the various guides, policies and information exchanges.

There may be disagreement between parents and educators over the values held by the early years setting. What is important is how to engage parents in a meaningful and mutually respectful dialogue. This may mean a huge investment of time and energy on the part of the educators in relation to individual parents. The easiest way to respond to racist parents is to reproach them for views and ostracise them, but it is also the most negative and unhelpful. If we see parents as true partners then we have to make a concerted effort to win them over to views that would benefit their child. It may be worth keeping in mind that many of our colleagues have had to work on their own racism before being able to provide an anti-racist environment. Parents are no different.

If educators are not confident about dealing with the comments or behaviour of racist parents they should work together to discuss and develop strategies for working with the parents. This would ensure that the parent/s received the same treatment on the matter from all the staff and enhance the confidence of the educator actually dealing with the parent. The same would apply if a child makes racist comments and the parents have to be called to discuss the incident/s. Parents' concerns should be listened to carefully and each argument or point dealt with directly and clearly. At the same time it is important to ask the parents some questions about the experiences that lead them to hold such views. This should help the educator to encourage parents to talk through their racist understandings. It is only when such understandings are clearly in the open that we can effectively challenge them and offer positive alternatives.

Each parent should receive a copy of the setting's equal opportunities policy and this should be used in discussions, where good educational reasons are offered to parents for why racism is damaging to all children. Early years educators might as well realise that it is only a matter of time before they encounter racist behaviour. It is best to be pre-emptive and deal with racism in parents before it surfaces. The setting's position regarding racism should be built into the information parents receive. A clear and thorough policy is essential. All parents should be informed of the policy when they first bring their child to the setting. Staff should also work out the strategies they will need for consulting parents and the best ways to involve parents in a regular review of their anti-racist work, as in all other areas of the setting's work.

All the groundwork for informing parents outlined here can be done in regular parental meetings. Use practical examples — for instance it is vital to explain the value of black dolls/images when introducing the toys in the setting. Similarly, when they are shown the posters, reading materials, puzzles, choice of topics or resources for the homecorner, parents should receive clear explanations of why we value dressing-up clothes from a range of cultures or why everyday images of black and ethnic minority people are important for the children's development.

Supporting black and ethnic minority parents

For their part, black and ethnic minority parents might also need help to deal with racism in our settings, or they may need support from the setting against racism in the community. If the ethos of the setting reflects a multiracial, multilingual society and the educators communicate their anti-racist values through handbooks and displays, it is more likely that parents will talk openly and seek support. Black and ethnic minority parents, along with all parents, should be supported in encouraging a positive self-image for their child at home. They should also have the opportunity to understand how the educators work at developing children's self-esteem in the early years setting.

Parental awareness can be raised through workshop-type activities, for example: using stories with them, showing them videos and discussing the issues raised, discussing the setting's criteria for selecting resources, or aspects of good and bad practice which promote or hinder anti-racism and how this might affect all children. Above all, parents should understand that there is no one right way to learn about anti-racism and that most people have to relearn their understandings of 'race'. It is useful for educators to know about the research on racism, so as to help parents realise the damage racism can cause. Through working with parents in this way we are also showing that we respect them and are pleased to invest time with them to negotiate understandings. It is inevitable that some parents will not be able to give up much of their time or even want to, but this should not affect the rights and opportunities of children to feel safe and secure from racism.

Cultural diversity and childrearing.

Concepts of childhood and child-rearing are all culturally and socially constructed. Each of these concepts may have different meanings across different cultures (Myers, 1992). Early years educators, particularly those working with very young children, should be acutely aware of this fact. Not much has been written about it and one of the few ways to find out what parents think and how this affects their child-rearing practices is through talking with them. The parents of a child are the best source of information about the behaviours and practices found in specific cultures.

Culture can be interpreted here in ethnic, class or gender terms. In single parent families, for instance, the way a father perceives or understands the way a child should be fed or disciplined may be different from the way a mother understands it. Although there might be individual differences in every person's understandings, some perceptions are held due to culturally specific.

These differences may lead to different expectations of the early years setting between educators and parents. Research by Yeatman (1988) found that some ethnic minority groups did not understand the difference between informal pre-school education and more formal schooling. These parents often assumed that their children should be involved in structured literacy and numeracy activities, not participating in learning through more informal play-way methods more commonly used in under fives settings. Parents and educators often base their understanding of what is happening to children in early learning settings on their own early experiences. That is why we need to explain the way we work and why to parents, and to create a dialogue in which parents can also explain their expectations. If we cannot meet their expectations we must be able to explain why.

Childrearing in early infancy varies across cultures and this too can lead to misunderstandings. For instance, parents who have recently come from the Indian sub-continent (most Indian and Pakistani parents are not in this category, likely to be born and bred in Britain) may still practice traditional childrearing. This may include viewing the mother-infant relationship as one of mutual pleasure where the child's needs are often met immediately rather than controlled. Examples illustrating these traditional practices include under threes-being fed and allowed to sleep when they want; less coercion during toilet training by parents content to wait until the child feels ready and wants to control herself; mothers massaging the child regularly with oils to strengthen muscles and skin tone, — time enjoyably spent for both mother and child.

The relationship between mother and child in British, western culture is in contrast determined to a great extent by the concern to time everything, controlling the child's feeding and sleeping patterns and toilet training. This can free the mother for other activities but may be due to a perceived importance in this culture to coerce children into becoming as independent as possible, as soon as possible. We should consider these alternative approaches not as better or worse ways of rearing infants but as culturally different. Although this different behaviour comes naturally to the parents and children it may cause difficulties for the educators, and for parents and children whose cultural practices are not recognised. As educators we too have culturally specific understandings of how children should be reared and this could become an area of conflict if communication between parents and educators is poor.

Robert Myers (1992) in *The Twelve Who Survive*, a study supported by UNESCO/UNICEF on strengthening programmes of early childhood development in the Third World, offers an excellent chapter on understanding cultural differences in child-rearing practices and beliefs. He illustrates how different practices evolve in different countries and how this is closely linked to the physical environment, patterns of settlement, economic and social organisations and the values and beliefs (often derived from religious beliefs) held by the group.

In many ways Myers (1992) challenges our ethnocentric view of child-rearing. Ethnocentrism is the application of views we hold — located in 'our' culture — as universal norms, without due regard to the existence of other cultural perspectives, other ways of viewing the world. A non-ethnocentric view of child-rearing would accept that there is no single blueprint but that there can be shared, overarching values, such as all children's need to have a secure, psychosocially stimulating caring environment. At the same time we have to accept that each of these values has different meanings for different cultural groups.

For instance, some educators may believe that children from impoverished rural backgrounds are more likely to be slow learners. It is true that children living in poverty are more susceptible to illness, but as Myers reminds us, if the child:

> is part of a family and a community which function in an integrated manner and which are intact and well-adapted to the local ecological and social contexts, that child is probably not 'at risk' in his psychosocial development. Yet the middle- income children living in a clean, modern home in an urban centre may be well-fed, immunised and free from disease without necessarily being in a situation that is positive for psychosocial development. (Timyan 1989, p.10; cited in Myers 1992, p.359).

So we should never fall into the trap of making crude assumptions based on children's backgrounds. We can always try and talk to parents to improve understandings all round.

Ethnic minority parents as educators to staff

Parents can provide the usual basic information about recipes, cooking, festivals and the like but their roles should be more than merely as cultural encyclopaedias. Besides we can get most of this information from books; these are not the only areas in which parents should be seen as helpers.

If we aim to provide a racial equality perspective in early years settings we must incorporate new experiences that are meaningful and relevant to the daily lives of children in the setting and to the wider community. It is certainly not about representing ad hoc, outdated, stereotypical or inaccurate information that will generate negative understandings of black and ethnic minority groups/children. As well as informing oneself of relevant research, up-dating staff training and having appropriate resources and learning material, it is vital to liaise with parents. They are the best sources of information about their child and their culture.

Such liaison not only benefits staff and children but also provides an opportunity to give respect and 'a voice' to parents who have traditionally not had much say in 'how' and 'what' children learn. It also ensures a balance of appropriate and representative cultural experiences for everyone in the setting. It will be a way for educators to learn that not all ethnic minority families relate strongly with an ethnic identity within their cultural group and that some ethnic minority groups are targets of greater racism. Some Bangladeshi families living in certain parts of London for instance, experience a great deal of overt racist victimisation, virtually every day of their lives.

Equally, within every religious group there will be huge variations in the way the beliefs are practiced and adhered to. Some parents may find it offensive if educators assume that they identify strongly with their ethnic group religion, cultural practices or beliefs. Only through a frank and open exchange of information can we begin to understand where they stand. Empathy is a good starting point. If we think about the variation within so-called 'British' culture we soon realise that there is no single version of Christianity, British food, dress or living styles and this is equally true of people we perceive to be from 'other' cultures.

Parents and their home language

Having learned from parents about the child's experience of language and which languages are used in the home, educators can consider which attitudes and skills need to be fostered in promoting the child's whole linguistic resource. Virtually all parents want their children to succeed educationally. However, they may have been led to believe from their own experiences that the best way to help their child to progress is to speak only English and drop their home language and culture.

Parents of bilingual children are usually delighted when educators explain that their child should maintain her home language/s. That, in fact, a sound grasp of the home language and culture can actually be an educational advantage (Cummins, 1984). As with other areas of the functioning and curriculum of the early years setting, written information on home language maintenance and educational advantage will be very helpful to parents.

There also needs to be a strong indication of commitment to multilingual education within the setting, to promote languages as a positive asset within families and within society. The role of bilingual staff is very important in this area and should be utilised both in the child's learning and in communication with parents. Chapter 3 on Language shows how parents can contribute to a multilingual learning environment.

SECTION III
Policies, Legislation
and Training

CHAPTER 6

Antiracism:
Policy Developments in
The Early Years

We have seen how complicated, inert, pervasive and subliminal racism can be in our society. Most organisations and groups that work for, and with, young children have recognised this fact and, to their credit, are making efforts to do something about it. The principle aim of this chapter is to highlight some of the efforts and processes by which some of the major UK early childhood organisations have achieved equal opportunities policies which include an anti-racist component. This chapter can offer only an overview, not comprehensive and detailed accounts of all the struggles to achieve this end. All the organisations mentioned continue to improve their anti-racism work. For up to-date accounts of their progress the individual organisations should be contacted directly —they are listed at the end of the book.

It would be naive to assume that early years workers alone can wipe out or dismantle racism, but most organisations and groups in the field recognise that if they are to give all young children the best possible start in life, they need to raise the awareness of their workers. They aim to do this by acknowledging that racism exists, alongside other inequalities, and initially to express their opposition to it through anti-racist or equal opportunities policies and then to further their commitment by putting the policies into practice. It is clear that most organisations begin with a policy to inform their work.

Take for example the following equal opportunities policy statement by the staff of Hillfields Nursery Centre in Coventry (see opposite). The policy statement is clearly an overall statement of commitment to an equality framework. This was, and is, seen as a starting point for the educators at Hillfields Nursery Centre and their many documents related to the practice and planning for the Centre would illustrate how this commitment is realised. However, it is impossible to illustrate how permeation of the equal opportunities policy statement has worked for the Centre without showing all their documents. It is sufficient in this instance to show how they started.

Why is policy important?

It is important for individual schools, under-fives settings, organisations and colleges to draw up their own policy statements. The process should involve parents, staff and others who use the service. This should be seen as the first step in opening up discussion and beginning a process of change (Chapter 4 elaborates on this issue). If the will exists to change an establishment, policy statements can show commitment, act as guidelines for staff conduct and begin the process of permeation of equal opportunities into the everyday practices of a setting.

A policy statement cannot be seen as an end in itself. Policy statements are sometimes written as an insurance against accusations of discrimination from insiders or outsiders, but without positive action to implement equal opportunities they become mere paper exercises, void of any effect. We have not 'done our bit' on equal opportunities by having a policy. The importance of a policy statement is not in the ownership of pieces of paper but in the discussion on equality issues, the ensuing change in practice, procedures, behaviours and structures which dismantle racism.

The policy statement is a beginning by which educators are given a code of practice and a framework for further practice development. It also acts as a public statement of commitment to providing an anti-discriminatory service. At the beginning it is helpful to remember not to be too

HILLFIELDS NURSERY CENTRE

EQUAL OPPORTUNITIES POLICY STATEMENT

WE RECOGNISE THAT PASSIVE POLICIES WILL NOT IN THEMSELVES PROVIDE EQUALITY OF OPPORTUNITY AND THAT SPECIFIC AND POSITIVE ATTITUDES AND APPROACHES ARE NEEDED.

STATEMENT OF VALUES

The Centre is opposed to racist and sexist attitudes and practices.

We are fully committed to the active promotion of equal opportunities in our employment practices, in our work in the Centre and in the provision of all our services.

People are of equal worth whatever their race, culture, ability, gender, social class or religion.

Though we believe all people are equal we must respect and value their differences.

We are determined to make all efforts to prevent discrimination against staff, families and children whatever their race, culture, religion, colour, sex and disability.

STATEMENT OF INTENT

To ensure that the Centre provides a welcoming environment to all users regardless of race, sex or disability.

The Centre will respect and be sensitive to ethnic and cultural diversity, stereotyping and disability.

Racist and sexist attitudes and comments will be challenged with staff, parents and children.

To ensure that all children have equal access to the whole curriculum.

Resources and displays will reflect and promote our anti-racist policy and represent gender and disability in a positive way.

HNC/1993

ambitious. Change will not occur quickly, particularly where educators wish to work and move forward together.

This chapter explores some examples of anti-racist policy formulation and development in a number of early years organisations and groups. An attempt is made to extrapolate the main themes, patterns and processes by which this work is progressing and offer conjecture on how this type of work could be advanced further. It is worth adding that the greatest progress in early years anti-racist policy writing has taken place in the 1980s and the real challenge for the 1990s and beyond is the implementation of these policies through the provision of adequate training and the continual re-assessment of curriculum offered to young children. Apart from Hillfields, only the policies of national organisations are cited. It is hoped that smaller institutions such as individual nursery schools, playgroups, combined centres, private nurseries and local childminders' groups will be encouraged to consider developing their own equality policies and practice in the light of the experience presented.

National Children's Bureau Early Childhood Unit

The Bureau is a national organisation which monitors all issues pertaining to the well-being of children, such as the effects of legislation, the role and status of care-givers in the home and in the community and international, national and local trends which influence children's lives, such as education, health, welfare and poverty. The Bureau collates information and resources and carries out research to inform those who work with children, policy makers and parents. The Bureau is funded mainly through government grants. It has an Early Childhood Unit which has a remit with particular focus on the under-eights.

The Unit describes itself as:

> ...a national centre for advice, guidance and information on current practice, thinking and research in the under fives field. It started work in 1986, and its implicit aims are to increase awareness of young children's needs, to raise standards of professional practice and to improve the provision of services for children under five and their families. The Unit works with policy makers, administrators, practitioners and researchers (Under Fives (now Early Childhood) Unit, 1990).

In the latter half of the 1980s the Early Childhood Unit set itself the task of developing a set of principles upon which to base its work and forward planning. They started their equal opportunities work as early as 1984, so as to inform and develop the set of principles which would guide their work. Under the director of the Unit, a small team of full and part-time workers established an anti-racist working group. Crucially, they recognised their lack of expertise in the area and co-opted members to the working group who had experience of working in the field of anti-racism, early years and policy development. They also acknowledged the need to have a black perspective by ensuring that the membership included South Asian and African-Caribbean representation. The working group met over about two years, and all members of the Unit met with the co-opted members. In addition to consultation and policy development the anti-racist working group raised awareness within the group and offered a half-day discussion session to the Unit's Advisory Group.

The anti-racist working group finally set itself the target for the Unit as a whole to adopt on-going anti-racist practices and perspectives throughout their work within one year. This was achieved and the working group was subsequently disbanded. During the whole process the Unit was supported by their Advisory Group, which was kept updated on the progress and development of the working group and any policy implications. At the same time the Unit's Advisory Group was also informed by black representatives. Interestingly, the Bureau's Management Board were by this stage also addressing the issue of developing an equal opportunity policy statement.

Of the National Children's Bureau's sixteen values and principles cited in their statement on 'Values and Principles' (NCB, Annual Review, 1992-1993) there are three which assert that:

— All children are of equal worth, whatever their ability, colour, ethnicity, gender, health, religion, sexual orientation or social class.

— We celebrate the richness and diversity of childhood, including the different strengths deriving from ability, age, colour, culture, ethnicity and gender.

— We seek to eradicate prejudice and discrimination against children as a group or because of colour, disability, ethnicity, gender, health, race, religion, sexual orientation or social class.

These are bold and laudable criteria and the Early Childhood Unit and the anti-racist working group recognised this. However, the Unit felt that an extension of earlier statements was necessary in order to develop a more positive and active stance toward racial equality. The following beliefs guide their work (NCB, Statement of Values, July 1992):

— Children are valued and their full development is possible only if they live in an environment which respects their individual identity, culture and heritage and positive action is taken to support this.

— We live in a pluralist society in which children will grow up in many different types and forms of family, reflecting a range of values and beliefs. We need to recognise and be sensitive to these, whilst acknowledging that the needs of children must be our prime concern.

So, there we have it. A process was on its way whereby statements of 'good' intent were being activated by belief and positive action, through the process of consultation, working group discussion, and a heightened awareness and committed standpoint by the Unit.

The Bureau, in addition to its work based on its Values and Principles statement, now have an Equal Opportunity Policy Statement which stands by its original principles but extends its statement of intent and responsibility for implementation. This is quite a step forward for the Bureau equal opportunities working party, as the statement of intent highlights:

The Bureau, recognising that passive policies will not in themselves provide equality of opportunity, acknowledges that specific and positive programmes of action are needed (June 1990).

The Bureau set itself a five-point planned strategy to combat direct and indirect discrimination in its employment practices, in the work it undertakes and in the services that it provides. To ensure that these intentions are implemented, the Bureau has made it the responsibility of every member of its Board of Management and all staff members to ensure application of its intent. Senior management are responsible for developing appropriate strategic and administrative application while the role of monitoring and evaluating the policy rests with the Equal Opportunities Committee. Lack of resources can hinder progress and the Bureau has therefore committed itself to ensure adequate financial resources for the training and other requirements that will be needed to implement the policy effectively.

As far as the work of the Unit is concerned, the staff have tried to incorporate equal opportunity targets into their annual forward plan. The Unit has a growing collection of specialist literature on anti-racism, anti-sexism and disability. Their packs and publications seek to ensure that equality issues permeate throughout. This is reflected in the materials supporting professional development in the 1990s e.g. *The Children Act Training Pack,* the *Young Children in Group Daycare* guidelines, the *Working with Children* curriculum pack and *Making Assessment Work* pack. In their 1990 publication, *A Policy for Young Children: a framework for action,* which advocates the need for an integrated early childhood policy for the nation. The Unit assert that any policy framework they advocate is guided by their values and principles statements. Three of these are:

— We celebrate the richness and diversity of childhood, including the different strengths deriving from ability, age, colour, culture, ethnicity and gender.

— Many services discriminate against some families in terms of culture, gender, class, and disability. Positive action, through changes in policy and practice, must be taken to address this discrimination.

— We seek to foster co-operation, collaboration and effective communication between those who work with and for children.

The Unit continues its work on racial equality within an overall equal opportunities framework, including through their joint conferences with the Early Years Trainers Anti-Racist Network, their focus in seminar and conference programmes on issues of equality and their involvement with the EEC-funded project 'Challenging Racism in Day Care', involving exchange visits to Italy, France, Belgium and Spain.

It is very reassuring that as part of an influential and national body the Unit is taking such a clear and unequivocal stance for racial equality. It is also salutary for smaller groups and institutions that positive outcomes are possible in this area. This is not to suggest that the process the Unit staff had to undergo to reach this potential was facile. A summary of any such lengthy process of change, such as the one for the Unit or the other organisations discussed, inevitably cannot do justice to the full extent of the struggles, setbacks or achievements within an organisation. This is particularly so when considering the process by which policies are implemented.

In the case of the Bureau and the Unit there have been many struggles over key strategies to ensure the implementation of their equal opportunities policy. The issues of networking with black and ethnic minority groups and the negotiation of the design of project work with funders has led to time- consuming dialogue. The issue of monitoring the progress of policy has also created some complex discussions. However, to go into detail on the setbacks experienced by one organisation may not be useful to others, because there is no blueprint for the 'right' way to approach change. Examples of different starting points and some of the promises and pitfalls organisations have encountered in their policy development can only serve to illuminate some situational similarities.

National Nursery Examination Board (NNEB)

The NNEB is an independent body which validates and regulates all NNEB courses including constructing the final examination for the certificate in nursery nursing. The courses are generic and available across Britain in about 150 private and local authority institutions of further education. The purpose of the courses is to train (usually young women) for child care work in several spheres of private and public employment, such as; any type of nursery, hospital, children's home, crêche, school or private home where children need care. Many nursery nurses go on to work as private nannies.

Although the NNEB is responsible for setting the final examinations, the Board does not prescribe a syllabus; rather it lays down regulations governing course objectives and a broad framework of guidance. However this framework may become tighter with the advent of the National Vocational Qualification (NVQ) for Child Care and the Board has already moved toward modular courses. Similarly the Board does not lay down strict criteria on access to courses, leaving these to the colleges. Under the current system some colleges require students to have two or more GCSEs, while others only require a pass in English or just go on the interview performance of the candidate.

In the 1980s the NNEB came under increasing pressure to review its guidance on policy and practice as far as issues of equal opportunities were concerned, in line with the increasing number of local education authorities which were adopting such policies. In 1986 Southwark Council for Community Relations and the ILEA Equal Opportunities Unit published the report *Nursery Rhyme or Reason*. It was the work of the working party on the care of the under-fives, whose remit it was to:

> report to the Education Officer on selection, training, employment and supervision of staff caring for the under-fives, with recommendations on the restructuring of existing provision to accord with the Authority's equal opportunities policy.

The authority in this case was the former Inner London Education Authority (ILEA). The working party found that, of the five colleges that offered the NNEB course, there was evidence of some inequality in the areas of course content, placements, access and the experiences of black and bilingual students.

As far as courses were concerned the report noted that:

> Grave doubts have been recorded as to the adequacy of the courses in preparing students to work in our multi-cultural, inner city life. Concern has been expressed about the omissions from the courses as well as about aspects that are included (ILEA 1986).

Much of this concern was over aspects that transmitted a deficit view of black families and treated them as pathological.

Black NNEB students were asked to give evidence of their experiences and this indicated that some NNEB tutors (usually white) needed urgent training in the area of racial equality, because it is hard to teach what one does not know. As one student put it:

> The lecturers were not aware of racism, to me they were not aware of the needs of black children and if they were then they did not show it. The white students...more than half of them were openly racist and I felt very sad to see that they were going out there to work with black children with their sort of attitudes...I know I wanted to pass the

117

examination so therefore I kept quiet or should I say, tried to stay quiet, but God it was hurtful. It was hurtful to me as a black woman, a black mother to hear what was being said about black women and their families (ILEA 1986).

Similarly some nursery headteachers felt that the focus on courses was more on issues of children's self-image and cultural heritage and that, although this was important, more was needed on exploring racism and its damaging effects on all children, black and white.

Similar problems were found in the area of recruitment, selection and retention of black students and in 1987 the Nursery Nurse Tutors Anti-Racist Network (now Early Years Trainers Anti-Racist Network — EYTARN), the National Child Care Campaign and the Commission for Racial Equality published a report based on a seminar for NNEB trainers on *Selecting Students: to ensure equality of opportunity* (1987). Over 80 participants from colleges all over the country discussed such issues as fair interviewing practice and the Race Relations Act. Reform of the NNEB policy and practice in relation to racial equality appeared to be urgently needed and the Board recognised this by establishing an Equal Opportunities Working Party to review its position across all areas of inequality. The Working Party had wide representation including senior members of the Board, members from education and NNEB tutors from various parts of the country. The Board had also been careful to co-opt black members who had some experience of young children and racial equality.

Although the Board's Working Party had taken on the admirable task of policy and review of equal opportunities in the widest sense — i.e. to incorporate 'race', gender, class, marital status, disability and religion — this also created a potential weakness. That is, one small group meeting approximately three times a year had to deal with every area without necessarily having the expertise, time or power to influence change effectively. This is not to suggest that the Board has not made progress in the area of equal opportunities. Quite clearly it has, but the progress has been slow and patchy, for instance over the issue of ethnic and gender monitoring in NNEB recruitment to courses.

As a validating and examining body, the Board has recognised its responsibility to have a policy statement concerning equal opportunities. The Board has also recognised that this is the first stage in the development of a long-term overall strategy, but the process by which the strategy is to develop is rather cumbersome. Nevertheless, it is commendable that the strong and committing words of their policy statement can act as guidance to those who are already committed in colleges to seek change for greater equity. The Board's policy in 1991 had six main strands, as follows:

(a) that it is committed to promoting equality of opportunity throughout its activities (this includes its employment policy and publications);

(b) that no applicant for a course of study leading to one of its awards should be disadvantaged compared with another by virtue of class, disability, gender, marital status, race or religion;

(c) that when considering the validation of a course of education and training leading to the Board's awards, the training institution concerned should demonstrate, as far as is practicable, a commitment to providing equality of opportunity including provision for the admission of students with a disability;

(d) that no student undertaking a course of study leading to one of its awards should receive less favourable treatment than another by virtue of class, disability, gender, marital status, race or religion;

(e) that in the assessment of students, both internally and externally, teaching institutions and the NNEB should ensure that no student receives less favourable consideration or treatment than another by virtue of class, disability, gender, marital status, race or religion; and

(f) that the curriculum for all its schemes should reflect a commitment to promoting equality in all the aforementioned aspects and so help to establish a concept of equality of opportunity amongst all sections of society (NNEB 1991).

The Board asserts that all who recruit, teach and examine for it should implement anti-discriminatory practices by ensuring that their attitudes, behaviour and day-to-day practices promote equality and, further, that any negative attitudes and behaviour should be changed. In terms of the curriculum, the NNEB's new modular scheme requires every student to complete a core 20 hour module on 'Equality of Opportunity'. This is a welcome initiative by the Board and highlights their commitment to the issue. However there are some problems with this approach.

Firstly, all the inequalities are to be dealt with together, and 20 hours will not be long enough to explore any one area in depth. Secondly, we cannot assume that all tutors are themselves aware of the issues, at least not enough to teach them confidently — I can recall many instances where conscientious tutors have argued for training for themselves in the area of equality. Finally, it will be very difficult for the Board to evaluate the success of the equality module or the permeation of the equality issues it advocates of all other modules, because there is no rigorous system of monitoring this area.

Although most of us would welcome the linking, understanding of and active participation against all forms of oppression, it is also disconcerting for those of us who are particularly concerned about racial equality (or any of the other inequalities) that some of the main issues are likely to be diluted. The process by which most people learn to make connections between inequalities is usually reached through the study of at least one area of inequality in some depth by a well-informed and committed tutor. Experience shows that racism, as the most 'uncomfortable' area of social injustice, is likely to get less than its share of attention. A student body composed mainly of women is happier exploring sexism. Given the lack of suitable training there is little chance that issues of equality will be dealt with in sufficient depth to alter the views or practices of many NNEB students. Equally, the chances of tutors teaching about racial equality effectively are limited unless there is substantial opportunity for training in the area. However, it is almost inevitable that the Board will not let the issues drop..

Pre-school Playgroups Association (PPA)

The Pre-school Playgroups Association is a national educational charity established over 30 years ago and the single largest provider of care and education for children under five. More than 15,000 playgroups are members of the PPA and over 628,000 children attend them (PPA, 1992). Given the large numbers of children and parents involved with the PPA, it is important to consider the PPA's position on the issue of racial equality.

Along with many other early years organisations seeking to improve equal opportunities, the PPA started thinking about racial equality in the late 1980s. PPA volunteers, staff and others within and outside the Association deliberated over how the PPA should tackle equal opportunities to eliminate discrimination and work toward ensuring equality in playgroups. The most pro-active work and publications have appeared in the early 1990s, which shows how the Association has followed confidence with action.

Initially the only reference to equality was in the Association's principles. Of the seventeen principles guiding PPA beliefs the last states that: 'There should be equal opportunities within the group for adults and children' (PPA, 1989a). The PPA's pink and green guideline booklets on *Good Practice for Full Daycare Groups* (PPA, 1989a) and *Good Practice for Sessional Playgroups* (PPA, 1989b) offer what appears to be an attempt at permeating practice with some guidelines on equal opportunities. However, these are separated and boxed under the title *Equal opportunities — Considerations.* This may leave some readers with the impression that the statements made under this heading in each section

are at best marginal and at worst optional. The positive aspect is that the issues are raised in each section and the PPA is making clear that equal opportunities is firmly on the Association's agenda.

If the guidelines are read alongside the Association's Equal Opportunities Policy Statements, the PPA's position on racial equality, gender and disability becomes apparent. Information sheet 5 (PPA, 1991a) is available from the PPA and is the Association's Equal Opportunities Policy Statement, beginning with the firm declaration that the PPA 'is committed to taking positive action to eliminate discrimination in all areas of its work' (PPA, 1991a). There are three statements, one on anti-racism, one on anti-sexism and the last on disability. The anti-racism statement is bold and asserts the following points:

> Because racism exists, this statement is being made to help us develop and put into practice anti-racist strategies. It is intended that:

1. Volunteers and staff become aware of racism, its effects and the implications for work.

2. The structure of the Association is amended so that it becomes more appropriate to the needs of ethnic minority groups and individuals.

3. Member groups are actively encouraged to provide an anti-racist environment and supported in doing so.

4. Within the aim of the Association, projects initiated by ethnic minority parents, organisations and communities are supported.

5. All PPA training is anti-racist in content and conduct.

6. The Association's marketing activities, which include public relations, publications and promotional goods, reflect our multiracial society and have an anti-racist perspective.

7. Recruitment methods are actively anti-racist and frequently reviewed. In addition, special provisions in employment laws are used to the full.

8. Employment situations are appropriate to all racial groups (PPA, 1991a).

The PPA's Anti-Racism/Equal Opportunities Development Group has continued its efforts to inform and influence practice through policy and publication. The PPA has freely available, for its membership and others, fliers which promote resources that support anti-racist strategies. More recently the PPA has published *Equal Chances* (PPA, 1991b), a book aimed at eliminating discrimination and ensuring equality in playgroups. The book directly addresses the area of anti-racist practice and asserts that equal opportunities are for everyone, highlighting that all-white areas have a responsibility to educate the children in their care about being part of a 'multiracial society'. Interestingly, the clear and strong references to racism and sexism so prominent in the Policy Statements are hardly ever mentioned in *Equal Chances*, which is predominantly multicultural, that is focusing on culture, ethnicity and diversity. The last two chapters of *Equal Chances*, however, are more about sharing power and taking action against discrimination and are therefore more anti-racist.

The anti-racist and equal opportunities lobby within the PPA have certainly devoted an enormous amount of energy and time to promoting

123

racial equality. It is to the Association's credit that so many of their publications are about or incorporate equality issues. According to the Association; 'All playgroup staff and parents in playgroup are encouraged to take short or longer courses' (PPA, 1992). It is to be hoped that racial equality perspectives and approaches are incorporated into all training, whether it be an initial 'Doorstep' course or the more advanced Diploma in Playgroup Practice. Anti-racist childcare training permeated throughout courses is the real test and what the PPA should aim to achieve.

PPA is one of the consortia of early years bodies making up the Council for Early Years Awards, which will be awarding NVQs from 1992. If the Association is serious about playgroup staff obtaining NVQs in Child Care and Education, their training must take into account the Underpinning Knowledge and Understandings (UKUs) required in the areas of equality. Playgroup leaders have to pay for their own training. This has serious implications generally but more specifically it may discourage some playgroup leaders from taking courses on racial equality. Particularly so, if they live in a relatively white area, and have not yet taken on board the fact that anti-racist childcare and education is critical in such monocultural locations. However the PPA encourage playgroup staff to try out the ideas in *Equal Chances* (PPA 1991b) and provide feedback on the positives, negatives and new ideas arising from practice, so that a second book can be written based on workers' practical experiences.

National Childminding Association (NCMA)

The NCMA has over 53,000 members and there are thousands of young children cared for and educated by their childminders every day. NCMA was founded in the mid-1970s and now has approximately 2,000 affiliated local childminders groups from England and Wales. Childminders care for small groups of children, usually in the home of the minder. This means that they can form very close relationships with the children in their care and influence the children greatly.

Like the other organisations mentioned in this chapter NCMA first set up its Anti-Racism Sub-Committee in the 1980s, in response to the concerns of some of its members about racial inequality. From the deliberations of this committee NCMA issued an anti-racist policy statement, which appeared on a flier with the bold heading:

Racism Damages all Children, White and Black: It disadvantages white children by giving them a false sense of superiority and a distorted picture of the world they live in.

This not only makes a strong statement but conveys the unequivocal message that racism is a white problem which damages all children. The anti-racist policy statement issued by the NCMA Anti-Racism Sub-Committee takes an assertive stance against racism. They state, as part of their policy that:

NCMA is committed to the development of an anti-racist childminding service which can respond fully to the needs of Britain's multiracial society.

Racism is the process by which Afro-Caribbean and Asian people as well as people from other ethnic minorities are denied equality status, power and access to power.

Racism is rooted in the belief that white people are superior to black people. This belief is not consciously held by all white people but it has been institutionalised in all the structures of British society including both national and local government, the education service and the provision of child care.

NCMA is committed to a childminding service which views children as different but equal and which strives to meet the needs of the whole child, physical, emotional, intellectual and cultural.

To this end, it is the responsibility of all childminders to acknowledge that racism exists, and that it harms all children in their care.

Good quality child care involves valuing each child equally and affirming the positive value of different skin colours, cultural and family backgrounds. It involves giving children a realistic picture of the world they live in and correcting the distortions and prejudices about that world.

Good child care is anti-racist child care.

Since the anti-racist policy statement, the NCMA has moved on to look at the effects of other inequalities and their policy is currently under review. NCMA has altered the name of its Anti- Racism Sub-committee to the Equal Opportunities Sub-committee of the NCMA. This is because, as NCMA suggest, anti-racism is just good practice. It is not uncommon for an organisation to realise that equality issues are closely connected and all need to be addressed. However, it is very difficult to address them all at once because although there may be many parallel strands, the specificity of each inequality, be it 'race', gender or disability, should not be lost. At the same time, gaining concepts in one area actually helps most people to transfer some of their new understanding to other areas of inequality.

NCMA will continue in its work on inequality and, as with other organisations, their major hurdle will be the transmission of vital equality principles to most childminders. This cannot be achieved without learning or training in this area. NCMA have held seminars and provided equal opportunities and anti-racist training for some staff responsible for the general running of the organisation. The next step will be to review how equality training can enter all training from pre-registration courses to the basic and other local courses.

What have we learnt?

There are many large and small organisations, from national bodies to individual care and education settings, which have embarked upon the same road to greater equality as those mentioned above, with varying degrees of success. The above organisations therefore do not represent a definitive list, nor are they necessarily the best examples. They are merely a sample of the organisations which have power and influence over the care and education of most of our youngest children and over those who work with them with regard to training, policy and practice. But there are important lessons to be drawn from the examples given.

Each of the organisations is involved in, and part of, a dynamic and continuing process of change and commitment towards racial equality (and other equalities). It is vital that this progress continues. Policies are very important, but the will and commitment of those in power to translate policy into practice is vital. There is no blueprint for the 'right' way of doing it.

The organisations that look at racial equality as a separate issue before drawing together other issues of equality appear to be more successful in understanding racial inequality and in expressing how they intend to move

their position forward in the area. They also appear to make better use of expertise and time, by calling upon experienced persons and groups for help and setting clear targets of achievement for the future. These often include the vision that progress can only be made in steps and that a process of continual reflection is crucial.

It is interesting to note that all the above-mentioned organisations started their thinking and actions toward racial equality in the 1980s. The real challenge for the 1990s is to what extent the policies will be put into practice. One particular dimension of this will be the willingness of organisations to prioritise racial equality as an area for training and continuous review. Who will train the trainers? How will issues of racial equality get onto the agendas of mainly white areas? What will be the procedures for evaluating and monitoring needs and progress? It is time we asked ourselves these questions and more, to help us learn from each other and to continue moving forward positively to transform the structures, powers and perspectives which hinder racial equality.

The way organisations or early years settings decide to monitor their performance in this area is vital. So far most organisations rely on internal membership to monitor their progress. Managers need to ask themselves if this is the most effective way of assessing their achievements and development or whether there is a need to involve colleagues from outside who may be less partisan. For instance, in order to achieve a greater sense of objectivity on publications, course content or recruitment, many of the above organisations have used outside 'experts' on issues of equality to comment on their work or become involved in the selection and interviewing of new staff.

The key question remains of how to monitor the role of management. The power differential between equal opportunities committees and senior management, whether in schools or other establishments, continues to be an area of tension, sometimes even when senior management is represented on the committee. One possible way forward may be the establishment of regular evaluations conducted by an external evaluator, or the establishment of a steering committee which from time to time reviews the work of the setting.

CHAPTER 7

The State in Three Acts

This chapter looks at how the Race Relations Act (1976), the Education Reform Act (ERA, 1988) and the Children Act (1989) all offer essential structures and contexts for developing racial equality in early years education and care. This is not to suggest that these laws are not open to criticism. There are many and these have been rehearsed by other writers in academic journals and books (e.g. Richardson, 1991; NUT Review 1989). We note some of the shortcomings, but the main objective of this chapter is to give you an outline of the central tenets of each Act and to help you draw out of the Acts what you can do; how you can use them positively to promote racial equality. While the ERA does not apply directly to children under five, many four year olds are now in primary classes and top-down pressure of the national curriculum on reception classes and pre-five settings is common (see for example; Sylva, Siraj-Blatchford & Johnson 1992).

The 1990s have seen, and will continue to see, unprecedented changes in the funding, structure and power of local authorities. These three Acts of parliament are being implemented alongside changes in legislation in housing, community care and social services, all of which affect families and children. The greatest changes have been in the speed at which legislation is implemented, the funding of services and the shift in power from local authorities to individual centres which provide the service to the community, for example, to individual schools, hospitals and other units of service provision. This is important at a time when funding is limited and previously taken for granted services that were provided under a locally funded system are now operating with separate budgets and within a market philosophy. The main problem is that services now have to cope with market fluctuations which will directly affect their budgets. For example, schools which are now given their budget according to the numbers of pupils on roll may now have to lose staff if the numbers of pupils on roll falls. This is very unsettling for both workers and managers. It also has implications for continuity and staff morale.

Institutional 'race' and gender bias in child care and education services

According to Flynn and Phoenix (1988):

> The legislation and local authority guidelines which govern the child care services have been created by white middle class people, with white middle class children and families in mind. The majority of Members of Parliament and the House of Lords are white men, as are those who hold senior positions of power in the public and private services and industry.

They argue that the guidelines have been created by people very unlikely to have experienced racism, who have grown up in a society that condones racism. They might well also have a particular view of what constitutes a 'family', and of the appropriate behaviours of family members. Recognising racism and supporting the full participation of women in the workforce are unlikely to be considered priorities. Most of the legislation affecting provision of services catering for young black children and their families does not recognise racism as an issue. However, we can try and make the best use of the legislation we have, firstly by understanding it, and secondly by using the parts of it which can help to bring about change for racial equality.

The Race Relations Act (1976)

The Race Relations Act (1976) is clear acknowledgement that racism exists in our society. It is the clearest piece of legislation which works for the elimination of racist practices. The Commission for Racial Equality (CRE) was set up as the statutory body responsible for enforcing the Act. Its purpose is to work towards the elimination of racial discrimination and to promote equality of opportunity and good relations between persons of different 'racial' groups.

In an effort to make the Act applicable to those working in the early years, the CRE has published a useful booklet entitled *From Cradle to School* (CRE, 1989). This outlines the main features of the Race Relations Act (RRA) as well as examples of discriminatory practice, and complements a similar publication entitled *Code of Practice: for the Elimination of Racial Discrimination in Education* (CRE, 1989) which refers directly to schools and other educational institutions. It is not necessary to read the entire Race Relations Act. Readers of this book would do better to read the two CRE booklets mentioned. They are easily available from the CRE (for the address, see end of chapter 8).

It is however worth highlighting the most salient points of the Act which are intended to guide employers, managers and practitioners in providing services free of racial discrimination. This should help workers in the field of early years to monitor and evaluate their services. The Act has implications for the way we recruit, train and manage the day to day running of our services. This relates particularly to equality of access to services, advertising, employment procedures, assessment and how we prepare ourselves to deal with racist behaviours and attitudes, since under the RRA it is unlawful to discriminate on racial grounds.

Jane Lane of the CRE has written widely about the uses of the RRA, and observes that 'Racism comprises many facets, one of which is that of racial discrimination. Under the Race Relations Act this is defined in four ways: direct and indirect discrimination, segregation and victimisation ' (Lane, 1990). She goes on to highlight how knowledge of these areas can illuminate our practice so that we provide greater equality. It is useful to look in more detail at some examples of practice which might be discriminatory.

☐ **Direct Discrimination** — most people would normally identify such examples as discrimination — they are the most conspicuous form of racism. Direct discrimination means treating one person less favourably than another on racial grounds, for example, refusing to employ a nursery nurse because she is black. This is unlawful. It does not matter whether the decision is intentionally racist or not; if it is unfavourable, it is unlawful. Similarly, admitting only white children or only black children to a playgroup would be unlawful. 'Racial grounds' refers to a person's 'race', colour, nationality, citizenship, ethnic or national origins.

☐ **Indirect Discrimination** — this refers to practices and procedures which have the effect of discriminating on racial grounds. Quite often this form of discrimination is unfair but not deliberate or intentionally malevolent. In *From Cradle to School* (CRE 1989) an example of allocating nursery or playgroup places to children by 'word of mouth' among parents is cited as a possible form of indirect discrimination if this procedure excluded children from a particular racial group. This can quite easily happen in a largely white area with a growing ethnic minority settlement, if parents who are part of an all-white playgroup continue to tell only their white friends of any new playgroup places. That way, no one new can break in. If the staff were aware of the need to scrutinise their practices in the light of community needs, such situations are easily avoided.

☐ **Segregation** — this comes under direct discrimination and refers to unlawful treatment through the segregation of children or adults on racial grounds. For example, separating children according to their racial background for group-work or play for no specific reason would be unlawful. Similarly, making nursery nurses who are black work only in multi-ethnic settings is likely to be found unlawful.

☐ **Victimisation** — If a person is currently taking action under the RRA on grounds that they have been racially discriminated against, they should not be treated less favourably. For example, it is unlawful not to consider a person's application to become a playgroup leader because they have previously complained about racial discrimination at the playgroup.

All the relevant sections of the RRA are outlined and discussed in *From Cradle to School* (CRE, 1989). These include very important issues and describe what constitutes discriminatory practices, including instructing others and applying pressure to discriminate. The booklet covers advertisement and employment procedures and explains how to provide services which are not discriminatory. It also describes a number of ways in which the RRA allows positive action on racial grounds. For example, it is permissible to take action to meet the specific needs of bilingual under-fives by employing bilingual assistants, or to employ strategies which positively encourage people from a particular racial group to apply for posts where members of that group are underrepresented. There has been a great deal of hot air on the subject of positive discrimination in the past few years. This is somewhat ironic in the light of the fact that white males have enjoyed such 'positive action' for centuries. It is vital that early years educators familiarise themselves with the relevant CRE publications and scrutinise their own practice accordingly. There is no matter of choice here, because legal obligations are involved and it is possible that some of our practices are unlawful.

The Children Act

The Children Act (1989) is a milestone in the history of protective legislation about matters affecting children. It is intended to improve the quality of life and recognise the rights of children. The Children Act provides a clearer balance between the protection of children, family autonomy and the role of professionals. The Act is underpinned by four main principles:

☐ **Parental responsibility** — this is an intentional shift away from earlier legislation which alluded to parental rights. It is assumed that meeting the needs of children is first and foremost a parental responsibility. However, although mothers and fathers are identified as the first to hold responsibility for their children, parental responsibility can be conferred to another person or body through a court order. The Children Act encourages partnership between parents and other carers in the best interests of the child.

133

☐ **Welfare of the child** — this is central and paramount in the Act. Law courts are guided by checklists to proceed in the interests of the child and without undue delay (Section 13).

☐ **Reviews of day care** — Section 19 makes it a compulsory obligation on the part of local authorities to review their day care services. This must be done every three years and the authority is required to review all their services providing day care for under eight year olds. For the first time this has meant that local authorities need to co-ordinate their review using the information available from education, social services and health authorities. These results are to be published and the authority is responsible for identifying future changes. Under Section 18 of the Act social services are required to provide childcare for children 'in need ' who are five and under and not yet attending school. This means, in effect, that local authority departments and voluntary organisations will have to collaborate and consult each other in relation to day care.

☐ **New registration system** — all individuals or groups offering childcare and education facilities for children under eight are required to register with their local authority social services department. This means that childminders, nannies and any other form of day care will have to be registered. Childminders and other educators cannot be re-registered if there is inadequate multicultural practice which does not cater for the cultural, religious or linguistic needs of the children under care. There are also mandatory conditions on the safety and maintenance of premises and equipment and numbers of children. Fees will be charged for each registration and for the compulsory annual inspection by the local authority. There is also discretion for local authorities to add other conditions. This adds considerably to the workload of day care advisers and social services departments.

Further details and training materials about the Children Act can be obtained from the National Children's Bureau and there are now several books published which are easily accessible from most bookshops, for example, *Blackstone's Guide to the Children Act* (1989).

Racial Equality and the Children Act

The Children Act is the first piece of childcare legislation which makes specific reference to racial equality, and because the legislation cuts across local authority departments and day care services for under-eights its potential to promote greater racial equality is considerable. The Act also places upon local authorities the duty to consider the racial group to which children in need belong, for example, in making arrangements for day care and in seeking foster parents. Where children have to be placed with foster parents they should be of the same religious persuasion as the child.

The clearest guidance to promoting racial equality is outlined in the Guidance and Regulations, Volume Two on *Family Support, Day Care and Educational Provision for Young Children* (Department of Health, 1991). This volume provides a framework to meet the needs of every child regardless of his or her ethnic background, precisely because the Act refers specifically to catering for children's racial, religious, cultural and linguistic backgrounds. During registering and inspecting day care facilities, local authorities will have the power to consider whether the care and education provided is 'seriously inadequate ' with regard to a 'child's religious persuasion, racial origin and cultural and linguistic background' (Section 74.6). If this is found to be the case the local authority can cancel registration and close that day care facility.

The duties of the local authority also require consideration of a child's religion, culture and language needs with regard to making any decisions about the child's welfare. The Act defines children 'in need ' as children with disabilities or those not likely to achieve or maintain a reasonable standard of health or development, or where these may become impaired without provision of services by the authority. But the Act warns that in the process of identification of children 'in need', care should be taken to avoid making decisions based on ethnocentric concepts of the various child-rearing practices of families in the community.

During the three-yearly review, data on the ethnic make-up of users of services will be matched against data gathered during ethnic monitoring of the population of the local authority. Local authorities will need to set up monitoring and evaluation procedures and guidelines to identify any racial discrimination and act to ensure equality to all groups. Any mismatch between practice and policy should be easily identifiable.

Implementing the Children Act to promote equality — what can be done?

The short answer to this question is 'Quite a lot, if we have the will'. However, it will take some local authorities more time and consideration than others because they start at different points . For example, authorities with a longer history of ethnically mixed communities may have a greater awareness of racial equality issues due to the work of anti-racist and community organisations, although this may not always be the case. Two distinct levels of change need to be worked at, the local authority and the early years settings.

At both levels practitioners and policy makers need to make sure that the 'race' equality aspects of the Children Act are well discussed and understood by their colleagues. Ideally this should be done with careful consideration of the Race Relations Act. If a proactive stance is taken and issues carefully discussed no-one should be in doubt of the legal requirements of the Act. Day care advisers in particular will need guidance from their authority on the criteria and objectives which should form the basis for judging racial equality in day care provision. A clear framework should aid anyone inspecting or registering day care services. The National Children's Bureau training pack for staff responsible for the inspection and registration of childminding and day care under the Children Act, produced by the Early Childhood Unit is a very useful resource. It is called *Ensuring Standards in Care of Young Children. Registering and Developing Quality Day Care* (1991) and is available from the Bureau.

Guidance on registration is vital. The Act requires that a carer is a 'fit person' to look after children. This person should be able to demonstrate a knowledge of multicultural issues and have a positive attitude to such issues and to people of different racial backgrounds. It is clear that support and training will need to be forthcoming at every level of our hierarchical authorities, because we cannot assume that those with 'power' automatically understand the issues. In fact, as we saw earlier in this chapter, it is quite likely that it is those higher up in local authorities who are likely to have even less experience of inequality. They may also require more training because of the influential positions they hold. Training should involve work on personal value and belief systems as well as providing information about the Act and workshops for developing guidance and criteria for inspection.

Local authorities are not always responsible for training. In the case of some of the voluntary organisations, such as the National Childminders Association and the Pre-school Playgroups Association, much work is already underway to provide satisfactory training on the Children Act and the requirements for the registration of childminders and playgroups. However, it will take time to reach the whole membership of these groups and other organisations of this kind. This suggests that the local networking of early years groups becomes an important vehicle through which extra training can be provided.

Given that there is now a statutory framework for racial equality in day care and education, it is clear that provision of services cannot be separated from the training required to run those services. Policy makers, trainers, practitioners, administrators and voluntary groups need to work together to define what is meant by the phrases 'religious persuasion', 'racial origin' and 'cultural and linguistic background', terms which recur throughout the Act. Without clear definitions, we will be unable to judge whether the criteria are met by our care givers. During registration and inspection the evidence for inadequate care needs to be clearly linked to the criteria to justify cancellation of any registration. Ideally, any decisions reached about the criteria and framework for registration should also involve elected members and lawyers. This task takes time and most local authorities are currently addressing it, under pressure due to the short time given to implement the Act.

At a more general level, training for racial equality and the Children Act should also be the responsibility of colleges that train teachers, nursery nurses and those that offer other courses on child care and education. Ideally it would be sensible to target training in the area of equality more generally. Issues of disability, gender and class are equally important and are mentioned in the Act. Taking all equality issues into account allows students to analyse the nature of oppression more generally and also to understand that inequality can effect a large proportion of the population. During local authority and college training workers should have the opportunity to confront and understand sensitive issues. Such as: why are there so few black carers? Why do some white carers avoid taking black children? Why do some black parents prefer white carers? Or even, why do we find this subject so difficult to talk about? Some of the answers to these questions can be found in Chapters one and two.

One thing is certain, if a local authority or training college feels that racial equality is an important area they will show this by allocating responsibility for racial equality to someone with the status (both personal and economic) and the commitment to implement it effectively. There are obvious and desirable outcomes possible from the Children Act, but there are also some hidden aspects which may not be immediately recognisable to everyone involved with day care. For example, the experience and perspectives of black staff are crucial to the successful implementation of racial equality. Black and other ethnic minority staff can offer valuable insights into the workings and effects of racism as well as providing invaluable information on childrearing practices, religious requirements of ethnic minority groups and knowledge about children's languages and early linguistic experiences. However, we must be careful not to exploit or make unreasonable demands of our black and ethnic minority colleagues, not all of whom may wish to offer their services as 'living encyclopaedias' on ethnic minority cultures!

The Children Act also makes it apparent that we do not have enough black or ethnic minority participation in our day care services. The experiences and perspectives of black staff are crucial and recruitment practices that lead to increased participation should be considered essential to progressive change. Another presently hidden aspect of concern this: Is someone who is racist towards a black or ethnic minority child is fit to be caring for any child? You or your colleagues might wish to raise and discuss other hidden agendas. At first sight this may seem a rather incrementalist vision, but coupled with the change in practice advocated above, which is now a legal requirement, we should see a greater shift towards racial equality.

There remain some major obstacles to be overcome. Firstly, local authorities need to demonstrate a commitment and will to integrate the required changes proactively into their registration and inspection of day care and to manage their three-yearly reviews keeping issues of equality high on their agenda. Secondly, the local authorities will need to find funds and time to ensure these changes are overseen and given proper consideration. Given the dire state of local authority funding and the sheer number of Acts and Bills they have to implement related to other areas such as housing, community care and education this will be difficult. One solution might be to address all areas together in relation to equality issues.

Finally — and this might not be as great a problem — local authorities will need to view provision and training together. If they do, it is to be hoped that they seek the most appropriately trained and informed people to manage the changes and resultant training.

The Children Act gives very clear guidance to local authorities on the basis for deciding on the fitness of an applicant in registration of a day care facility and the Act requires applicants to be informed of the criteria being used to judge them. Two of the ten requirements are:

— knowledge of and attitude to multi-cultural issues and people of different racial origins;

— commitment and knowledge to treat all children as individuals and with equal concern.

This cannot be achieved without the full backing of trainers within the local authority, voluntary organisations and colleges. Individual responsibility to seek out existing good practice and further training is also needed.

Education Reform Act

The Education Reform Act (ERA) (HMSO, 1988) is applicable to England and Wales. In the first chapter, dealing with the curriculum there is an optimistic statement on the very first page which appears to bode well for racial equality. It states that schools should offer: 'a balanced and broadly based curriculum' which:

(a) promotes the spiritual, moral, cultural, mental and physical development of pupils at the school and of society; and

(b) prepares such pupils for the opportunities, responsibilities and experiences of adult life.

Unfortunately this statement is one of the very few glimmers of hope in the ERA, as we have seen, particularly in the chapters specifically concerned with promoting a curriculum for racial equality with young children.

139

What is the purpose of the ERA?

The ERA is rooted in the philosophy of the market economy and has three main aims: Firstly to raise educational standards, which are alleged to be low in comparison with our industrialised European counterparts. Secondly, to give parents more power to choose the school they consider most appropriate for their child and to have access to regular school reports on their child's educational progress. Thirdly, to make schools and teachers more accountable to parents and society by giving them control over a large part of their own budget under the local management of schools (LMS), and by giving parents a 'parents' charter' which outlines what information they can expect from schools.

In this scenario the parents are clearly the consumers or clients and the schools are the service providers. In this respect, in theory at least, the parents can choose where to send their child to school. Schools are funded on the basis of the number of children admitted and apart from nursery age children the younger children in the statutory school sector (that is, five to sixteen year olds) are allocated less money than older children. The reasoning behind this is unclear and one can only assume that it must be because they value secondary school children more than primary school children. The government has encouraged schools to 'opt-out' of local authority control and become even more independent financially and educationally.

However, as long as a school remains within the state sector all children in the statutory age group must follow a national curriculum and provide religious education of a 'broadly Christian' nature. Independent schools and public schools are free of these constraints. While children are in school they will be tested four times, at the ages of 7, 11, 14 and 16. The test results are published and parents receive these in the form of an individual report on their child. Schools' overall results have been published in the press as 'league tables'. Sweeping changes have also been made in further and higher education.

The ERA has profoundly reduced the power of local education authorities. The major funding, policy and administration duties have been delegated to schools, where most of these decisions become the responsibility of the headteacher and the school governors. The Act also abolished the Inner London Education Authority (ILEA). ILEA was the largest authority in the country and one of those with strong policies and monitoring procedures for equal opportunities. The resources produced by ILEA are still used nationally in training and by schools, and many of these are concerned with equality and inner city issues. It is worth looking more closely at how these structural changes affect issues of racial equality. There is absolutely no mention of equality issues in the ERA, although certain National Curriculum Council related documents provide guidance which can be used positively. But we should not be unaware of the negative aspects of the ERA in relation to racial equality.

The National Curriculum

The ERA describes the national curriculum as a basic 'entitlement' for every child to a broad and balanced curriculum. Both as a sentiment, and as a legal requirement this is to be welcomed. All children regardless of their ethnic background or knowledge of English are entitled to full access to the curriculum. The national curriculum is made up of nine subjects. The core subjects are English, mathematics and science, and the foundation subjects history, geography, technology, music, art and physical education. In Wales there is a tenth subject: in Welsh speaking schools Welsh constitutes another core subject and in non-Welsh medium schools a foundation subject. In addition to this a modern foreign language is to be taught in secondary schools. Religious education is also a compulsory part of the school day. The ERA directs that each state school should arrange for a daily act of collective worship which 'is of a broadly Christian character'.

Parents have the right to withdraw their children from assemblies and can apply to their local authority Standing Advisory Committee on Religious Education (SACRE) for alternative religious education and worship, for example, a Jewish or Islamic assembly. This is a sad situation for many infant schools where there has been a growing tradition of collective assemblies which allowed classes to share and celebrate their integrated topic work. Children would sing and hear stories from a range of religious faiths but this multi-faith approach is now being denied many children. It is questionable whether very young children of four to seven can really understand or benefit from the kind of religious instruction required by the ERA.

The curriculum is a powerful tool through which children learn the values of a society. Britain seems to be trying to emulate the education

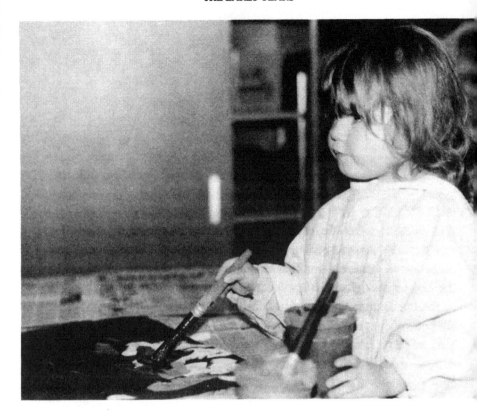

systems of countries that are admired economically and ideologically, but these countries might not in fact be the best educational role models. We are in danger of losing sight of other qualities, such as the social and emotional well-being of people, the importance of the environment, or the aesthetic and spiritual needs of human beings, all of them important to the education of our future citizens.

The National Curriculum Council (NCC) and the Schools Examination and Assessment Council (SEAC) have recently been merged to become the Schools Curriculum and Assessment Authority (SCAA). This body is responsible for schools' delivery of the national curriculum and the development of the tests to be taken by children. We are assured that there will be regular monitoring and evaluation of the national curriculum and that teachers' views about the workings or problems of the new curriculum will be welcome. There is no reason why suggestions on improving the national curriculum to promote racial equality should not be submitted to SCAA for consideration.

According to Janet Donoghue (1991), a Professional Officer at the NCC, equal opportunities should be a central feature of the curriculum. Donoghue argues that the national curriculum does not constitute the whole curriculum and that cross-curricular dimensions and themes need to be considered. The NCC has outlined a number of cross-curricular themes such as citizenship, health, careers, environmental and economic awareness, as well as multicultural and gender issues. The NCC states in its newsletter (NCC, 1991) that the:

> NCC does not see multicultural education as a 'subject ', but as a dimension which permeates the entire curriculum. As such, it should be at the heart of curriculum planning, development and implementation. Council is drawing on the work of its Multicultural Task Group to ensure its publications and activities take this dimension fully into account.

In spite of these reassurances to publish something of use to teachers, the NCC never produced anything specifically to guide teachers on racial equality in education. Donoghue (1991) claims that the entitlement set out in the ERA includes:

— treating pupils as individuals, meeting individual needs and valuing individual contributions;

— providing equal access to the curriculum and other aspects of school life;

— challenging myths and stereotypes.

Equal opportunities issues feature in every aspect of school life, apply throughout the curriculum and are the responsibility of all teachers.

Some aspects of the national curriculum undoubtedly lend themselves to promoting racial equality. The English orders make reference to promoting an awareness of other languages and the present technology orders advise that consideration be given to technological advances made outside of Europe and the West. There are many more examples from the other subjects, but it requires a skilled and well informed teacher to be able to translate the orders into a practical teaching context. Because of the slow and grudging pace at which the NCC worked on this matter, the Runnymede Trust (a charity dealing solely with 'race' issues) under the directorship of Robin Richardson, set up a working party which has produced a document entitled *Equality Assurance in Schools: Quality, Identity, Society* and published by Trentham Books (see address in last chapter). *Equality Assurance* will help those working with young children in schools to deliver the national curriculum with a racial equality dimension.

For educators who remain unaware of the issues and have no commitment to racial equality, the national curriculum will not restrict their ethnocentric practices so will disadvantage the children in their care. Any parent can challenge their school to provide evidence that they are incorporating the cross-curricular themes and dimensions mentioned above throughout the basic curriculum. Schools are required by law to do this, but it will be difficult to implement because it does not form part of the assessed elements of the curriculum.

School assessments and black and ethnic minority children

Every child is entitled to be tested, that is, to complete the Standardised Assessment Tasks (SATs), even children whose English is still at an early stage of development. Circular 11, published by the NCC on Linguistic Diversity, advises teachers on how to assess bilingual children, including using bilingual assistance for assessing maths and science, though not English. This is helpful to black and ethnic minority parents, especially those who feel that their children's academic progress was not taken seriously or satisfactorily reported to them.

Parents have also been extremely concerned about the disproportionate number of black children excluded temporarily or permanently from school. At least under the entitlement of the ERA it is the duty of the local education authority to ensure access to the national curriculum, even for those excluded from school.

How ethnic minority and black children have been assessed has always been a matter for concern. The ERA requires that teachers use teacher assessments as well as SATs to measure children's overall academic achievements. Patricia Murphy (1989) has demonstrated that even when teachers know that tests and assessments might be culturally biased they do not identify the bias, because they have not been trained to do so.

If our knowledge is 'racialised' in favour of certain groups, then for educators to remain unaware of how this affects assessments is almost bound to work against ethnic minority groups. As Murphy says:

teachers are cautioned about the problems of bias yet no account of it is taken in the selection and organisation of curriculum content. It is commonly assumed that a national curriculum ensures equality of access, but pupils will not have equal access to knowledge if the curriculum provision they receive fails to validate their experiences and ways of 'making sense' of the world (p37, 1989).

In other words, it does not matter how broad and balanced a curriculum is; if it holds no cultural relevance for the child then she is unlikely to perform to the best of her ability.

Teacher education and training

The ERA has had severe impact on the training of teachers. The sheer amount of subject knowledge and the wide range of subjects allows very little time for students to study the influences of social factors on learning. This aspect of teacher education was traditionally undertaken by teaching studies departments. Tutors in these departments brought together issues of child development, effects of the environment on learning and the relevance of subject content and the methods and strategies used to teach it. This part of teacher training is being squeezed out, under the pressure to transmit more subject knowledge. It might be logical for tutors in science or the arts to begin incorporating teaching studies into their teaching about the subject — and of course some tutors do so already. However the majority remain as ignorant as their students on the matter of equality issues.

The implications here are twofold. Firstly, divorcing subject content from equality issues misinforms students, so that they are likely to deliver an ethnocentric version of the national curriculum. If the major part of training is transferred into schools, the same problems will apply: students allocated to teachers who have little or no understanding of equality issues will see little connection with their subjects. Secondly, if black and ethnic minority students do not have their special skills e.g. their multilingualism or their understandings of particular ethnic minority cultures valued positively, they may never use these assets in school.

Local Management of Schools (LMS)

Instead of being managed by the local education authority, under LMS schools manage themselves. This may sound desirable but there are many hidden problems. LMS is designed to make schools more competitive. Schools are allocated funds according to the number and age of children. LMS provides no extra funds to support children's particular needs. If a school has a large number of children whose mother tongue is not English there is no extra fund for staff to support them. Similarly if there are disproportionately large numbers of children who have special needs, such as behaviour problems, learning difficulties or are 'gifted', there is no extra financial support. Children who are seen by an educational psychologist and subsequently 'statemented' may be eligible for extra support, but the LEA has to find this extra funding, and given the constant erosion by central government of local authority budgets, this is often impossible.

The way the formula for delegating funds to schools is operated can disadvantage schools with black and ethnic minority children. For a start, most primary schools with large numbers of black children on roll are in inner city areas. Apart from suffering from the normal inner city problems, such as living in poorer housing and suffering greater unemployment and poverty, children in these areas may require greater emotional and cognitive support. In particular they may need more experienced teachers, bilingual resources to support English acquisition and, in the early years (4-5 year olds), a lower ratio of staff to pupils. Under LMS, experienced teachers and extra staff and resources may simply be too expensive for the school's annual allocated budget. If the number of children on roll falls cuts have to be made, and schools might well lose their nursery nurse from the reception class or sacrifice an experienced teacher for a cheaper, younger and less experienced one, or cut the budget for learning resources.

The Parents' Charter

All parents want the best education and care for their children. The parents' charter has been issued by the Department for Education (DFE) informing parents of their rights concerning schools. It is interesting that there is no national charter for children. To date, the only children's charter is that produced by the Lothian Regional Council. This area of Scotland has broken new ground by recognising that children should have rights too. The *Lothian Children's Family Charter* (1992) covers more than education, including also children's rights within the family. The parents' charter is intended to increase parents' awareness of the kind of information they are entitled to from schools and thereby increase their ability to choose between schools.

The charter informs parents about their entitlement to have regular progress reports from their child's school and gives brief details of the national curriculum and assessment procedures. It encourages parents to judge a school by its overall academic results. This is bad news for schools that perform less well academically compared with their neighbouring schools in more 'advantaged' areas. There are two reasons why this is a problem. First, schools that perform badly according to published league tables might actually be successfully raising the academic achievement of their pupils, but because it is only final outcomes and not, as it should be, the *progress* each child makes that gets measured, the possibly considerable achievements of some schools go unrecognised. Secondly, schools themselves may feel pressured not to admit children they rate as 'slow' learners because these pupils' test scores might affect the school's position in the 'league tables' results and reduce their popularity.

Many of us are beginning to hear disturbing stories of children who are not admitted to schools for such reasons. In one largely white area of the country a multicultural advisory teacher is receiving complaints that certain schools are refusing to admit four and five year olds simply because English is not their mother tongue. The schools have argued that they do not have the funds for the extra resources required or suitably trained staff and that 'these children' will bring down the academic scores of the SATs in the tests on seven year olds. Of course, these things rarely appear in writing and this makes it difficult for the LEA or ethnic minority parents to use the Race Relations Act to bring actions against the particular schools.

All early years workers, teachers and parents need to know about the three Acts we have discussed, if they are to exercise their rights successfully on behalf of the children in their care. If they do not set out to inform themselves of the new legislation, we can expect middle class, articulate and mainly white parents to remain disproportionately — and increasingly — advantaged.

The role of Governors

The ERA has allocated governors increased powers over the financial, legal and administrative running of schools. This includes the hiring and firing of staff and the overseeing of the delivery of the national curriculum. Governors are not paid for these duties and meetings often take place in the early afternoon. Both these conditions disadvantage working class and black and ethnic minority governors, because they are likely to be poorly paid and have to work long hours.

Governors have increased powers yet they tend to be the people least likely to see the need for multicultural or anti-racist practice. Schools no longer have to adopt their LEA policy on multicultural or anti-racist education so it is up to the governors and the school whether they pursue and implement these policies. In the mid-80s over 80% of LEAs had policies on equal opportunities. It is going to be very difficult to ensure that schools continue to promote this area of their work. Many local authorities recognise that they need to provide anti-racist training for their governors and many are actively doing so. The main problem still remains with the white and more rural areas, where awareness at a school level still remains fairly poor.

CHAPTER 8

Training and Resources: The Way Forward

Families and staff are the key resources for a centre implementing a multicultural perspective. However, many centres find it difficult to implement a multicultural perspective because they lack resources, energy, time or expertise. Similarly, centres that are implementing a multicultural perspective need guidance, new ideas, time to reflect and to assess what they are doing. (Stonehouse, 1991, p.82)

The 'E' in Equality

Equality issues should permeate the whole setting's policies, procedures, practices, behaviours and structures. But this cannot happen without careful planning and training. Some educators argue that they have an enormous job without adding equality to their agendas, but it is not a matter of 'addition'. If we are concerned with the whole child, the whole curriculum and the need to provide a quality service to families and children — as all early years settings are — we cannot ignore equality issues. Quality constitutes seven eighths of the word equality and without equality issues at the head of our agendas and workplaces there will be little real quality in our provision.

In a recent workshop run for the National Children's Bureau I asked a group of early years specialists what kind of training early years workers needed for the changing 1990s (see p.151). These specialists included workers from the fields of education, care, voluntary and private sectors. I called on them to identify key attributes and learning needs for workers under the headings: 'attitudes', 'skills' and 'knowledge'. They agreed that it was impossible to argue for high quality provision for young children without high quality training. The diagram opposite maps out the findings of the group and some of the interconnections made. It shows how equality issues are integral to good practice. It would be interesting to carry out similar activities elsewhere to highlight the training needs of educators.

Ourselves — a good starting point

The first step to racial equality in early years settings is to recognise that educators are not objective, value-free beings. In fact, we are quite the opposite — our life-histories make us highly subjective and our actions are always value-laden. It is interesting that Stonehouse (1991) and others quite often write about a 'multicultural perspective', yet their guidance deals with issues of prejudice and racism. Many writers view the use of terms such as racial equality and anti-racism as antagonistic to the 'softly-softly' approach they recommend.

Stonehouse (1991) is quite correct in suggesting that we have to overcome a number of obstacles before we come to realise the sort of educational context we want for our children. The most difficult obstacle most of us face is knowing where to start. Starting with our own consciousness and awareness of racial equality issues is probably the best way forward.

Terminology is an important factor in realising our goals and determining what we stand for. For instance, Dermon-Sparks (1989) hinges her work around the anti-bias curriculum. Taken literally, the term anti-bias makes little sense, because every statement, utterance and action we take is biased. Does that mean that we are anti everything? Of course not! Some of our biases, our advocacy for children for example, are positive, other biases maybe less so. The important thing to acknowledge is that all knowledge and commitments are biased and that our aim should be to weed out the biases which are harmful or counter-productive to the well-being of young children and to our multi-ethnic staff and community.

HIGH QUALITY PROVISION REQUIRES HIGH QUALITY TRAINING

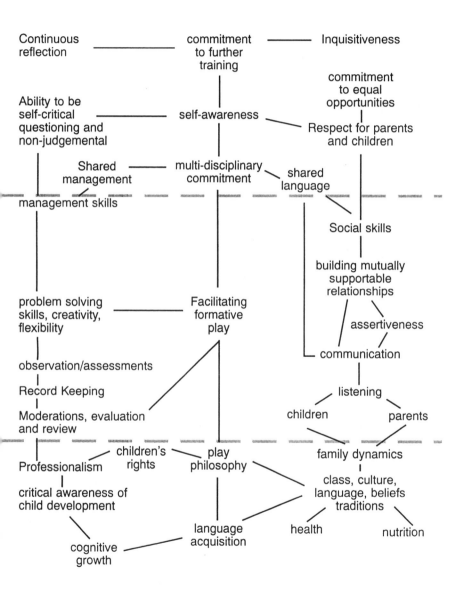

We should state clearly what we stand for and take care with the words we use to describe our actions.

Keeping racial equality in mind, staff can usefully explore the tensions they feel on this issue by drawing up personal retrographs (time-lines) of their life-history (see diagram opposite). The retrograph could include events in their lives as well as significant periods or moments of learning and any critical incidents which have led them to hold the values they cherish today. No one should have to share any part of their life which they consider too personal or painful to share. There will be enough information without it to stimulate a good discussion on how we become what we are, and why we believe and feel the way we do about certain issues. Most importantly the activity will provide a concrete demonstration of the on-going 'constructed' nature of individual and group identities. Such a recognition may be an essential prerequisite to fully accepting our role in contributing to the construction of our children's identities.

This activity must be led by someone who cares about the feelings of the staff and is capable of handling sensitive information gently. Sessions such as these can sometimes be painful and yet they are very rewarding, providing us with new understandings about why we hold the attitudes that we do towards black and ethnic minority people. However, this should not be the sole aim of the activity. Issues of gender, class, disability and sexuality can also be raised and these too have to be considered in the fostering of equality.

It is not only what is experienced in life that contributes to our attitudes but also what is omitted, what we do *not* experience. For instance, there may be staff who lived only in white middle class areas and went only to white middle class schools. The group facilitator would need to draw out the implications of such an upbringing. Conversely, if there are black and ethnic minority educators in the group, they may raise issues of overt and hidden racism which will also have to be discussed sensitively.

Another activity which can help us to explore our background is the issue of ethnicity. It is sometimes forgotten that everyone has one! Educators can be encouraged to define what the word means and explore what their own ethnic origin might be. In sessions of this kind I have been interested to observe that many students and educators make comments related to where they were born or bred, for example 'I'm Welsh', 'I'm from the North', 'I'm a South Asian from East Africa'. Others refer to

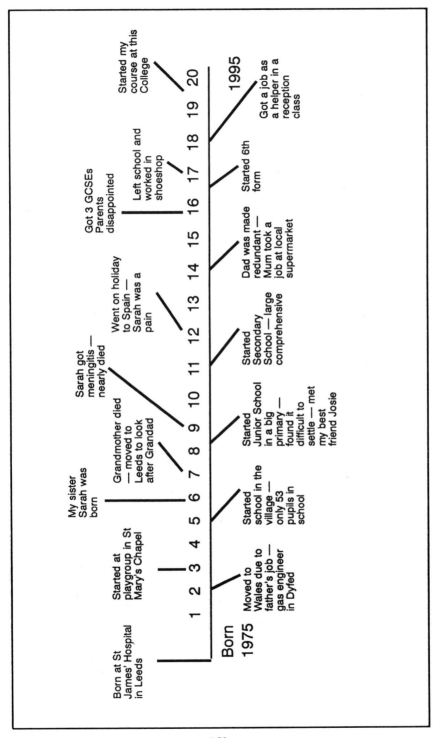

Born at St James' Hospital in Leeds

Started at playgroup in St Mary's Chapel

My sister Sarah was born

Grandmother died — moved to Leeds to look after Grandad

Sarah got meningitis — nearly died

Went on holiday to Spain — Sarah was a pain

Got 3 GCSEs Parents disappointed

Left school and worked in shoeshop

Started my course at this College

Born 1975

Moved to Wales due to father's job — gas engineer in Dyfed

Started school in the village — only 53 pupils in school

Started Junior School in a big primary — found it difficult to settle — met my best friend Josie

Started Secondary School — large comprehensive

Dad was made redundant — Mum took a job at local supermarket

Started 6th form

1995

Got a job as a helper in a reception class

1 2 3 4 5 6 7 8 9 10 11 12 13 14 15 16 17 18 19 20

their religious background, such as, 'I'm Jewish and I've always felt a bit on the fringes', 'I'm a Muslim' or 'I'm a Seventh Day Adventist'. Yet others will refer to their roots, 'I was brought up in Britain but I'm seen as a Jamaican' or 'I feel like I'm an Indian, because I was brought up that way'.

Statements of this kind (all have actually been made in sessions) can generate interesting discussions on what constitutes ethnicity. Myths about 'ethnics' as 'others' can be deconstructed and more factually correct information provided. We all have an ethnicity and it is formed by our multiple identities. For example a person with African-Caribbean parents, born and schooled in Scotland and further educated and settled in England will identify with all the geographical areas and the cultures related to these areas.

So we begin to see the multiplicity of human experience and our own position regarding ethnic and racial identity, and that it is important for every person. Learning about ourselves — ethnicity, racial identity, dress, religious belief, the food we eat, our gender and how this impacts on our (and others') behaviour, educational background, the expectations of others and their effect on us — are just some of the ways into learning more about our attitudes and allegiances. This learning can also provide clues to why it is difficult for us to take on new ideas that are based on the experience of others. It can certainly help educators to begin to discuss issues such as stereotypes, prejudice, racism, sexism, power, equality and justice.

Training activities for educators

To educate a whole staff to adopt racial equality perspectives in an early years setting requires careful planning and structure. The structure should be planned together and the process seen as a joint venture. For students on NNEB or teacher training courses (or others) this might be difficult because of the set syllabus for looking at equality issues but tutors should be flexible and incorporate students' perceived needs as far as possible. The following is not a blueprint for the development and support of an anti-racist perspective but could be adapted to meet the needs of individual settings and multi-professional groups. Settings within a geographical area could have joint training or at least support each other by meeting regularly.

1. Include all the staff in planning a series of staff development meetings

Most settings have a programme of in-service training so it is vital that staff are consulted when drawing up a development programme for racial equality. The staff development programme should be negotiated, to foster joint ownership of the whole process from the beginning. Ideally, some or all of the sessions should be open to all staff, including ancillary, education and care staff. Senior staff should take a lead and show their commitment by making the time and committing other resources and energy to the programme. A key member of staff should be allocated responsibility for co-ordinating the programme.

This should be a member of the senior management team. At the very least, a member of staff committed to change should take on the work but liaise regularly with a senior member. The programme should include clear objectives and targets to be reached over a period of time, say one year, and the issues to be covered should be identified and prepared for well in advance of regular meetings.

2. Getting started with the educators and ancillary staff

Opportunities should be built into the programme for staff to explore their attitudes as shown in this chapter. Time will need to be loosely structured as staff will need to explore some difficult concepts, such as: personal racism (either as victims or perpetrators), how they may unwittingly have promoted racism and the meaning of terms like equality, ethnicity, racial identity, culture, justice. While the development programme is taking place 'social dramas' or incidents might occur in the setting which need immediate attention, for instance, racist name-calling. Make it clear to all staff that the views of everyone, including secretaries and caretakers, contribute to the kind of ethos a setting has.

For example, in one setting a caretaker discovered racist graffiti on the walls near the entrance of the early years setting and removed it immediately, before parents and children began to arrive. He saw it first thing in the morning and he informed the head of the setting as soon as she arrived. He had participated in the training programme on anti-racism. He was sensitive to the feelings of the parents and did not want them to see such appalling slogans on the setting walls. He had noted details of the wording

155

'We don't have a problem in this playgroup because we haven't got any of 'them' here'.

'We don't have a problem because we only have two 'ethnics' in this Year One class *and* both their parents are professionals'.

'It's OK to learn about other cultures in nurseries but we must be careful not to go *too much* the other way'.

'I don't see why I should change my childminding practice. After all, 'they' chose to come here and should fit in with this country'.

'I don't see what all the fuss is about — young children don't notice colour so why should we?'

'This is just another fad. We don't have to get on every bandwagon, it will have its day and be forgotten'.

'Racial attitudes come from parents and it wouldn't be right to set children against their parents'.

'It's wrong to draw children's attention to skin colour — that will only make things worse'.

'The problems all come from the media and the local community — there's nothing that *we* can do about it'.

— Further examples may be taken or adapted from the 'Assumptions Exercise: 57 Varieties' in *Multi-cultural Education* by John Twitchin and Clare Demuth, BBC 1985 (p.185-194).

and type of spray used, to pass on to the police who were called in. The staff all agreed that he had taken the right action. This illustrates the kind of ethos that positively combats racism. In another setting where the staff had tried to create an anti-racist ethos but neglected to involve ancillary staff, the secretary was overheard reprimanding a four year old South Asian boy for his way of eating. She told him that only animals ate with their hands. She was obviously unaware of eating practices within the community, so damaged the boy's self-concept and offended the community group he came from. This incident acted as a 'social drama' which raised the awareness of staff and the secretary was included in the staff programme.

Exploding the myths behind commonly held beliefs about black and ethnic minority groups is also a valuable source for discussion. White educators have been heard to make the kind of statements set out opposite.

A number of such statements can be written on cards and given to groups to discuss, sort and report back on. The biggest problem is that members of a group may feel comfortable with these statements and might have made such remarks themselves. They may already hold the view that anti-racist education is solely for black and ethnic minority children. It should be clear from the foregoing chapters that this is not the case; anti-racist education is for all children and particularly for white children, who may grow up to be perpetrators of racism if we do not show them alternative ways of thinking and behaving. Part two of the book has dealt with this issue in more depth. However, the role of the trainer is to allow groups to discuss the statements and then to explain how the beliefs in the statements are prejudicial and can lead to racist discrimination.

3. Look at the setting's policy and philosophy

Attitudes to the education and care of children will have been determined by earlier outdated values and will have shaped the setting's policies and philosophy. As awareness of issues related to racial equality grows, staff may want to make changes to their documents. For instance a policy on language development might not have recognised the need for multilingual awareness in the setting for parents and children, nor the need for clearer criteria for selecting books which are not racially biased and so misleading and offensive.

Similarly, there may be gaps in policy, for example on how to deal with racial harassment, in terms of procedures for children, staff and parents. The mechanisms for new procedures for dealing with behaviour, for ordering new equipment and resources for the setting or for supporting and educating parents about racial equality may have to be re-evaluated.

4. Establishing an equal opportunities loan library

Staff development sessions in themselves might raise a great deal of awareness but it is unlikely that they can provide educators with all the knowledge they require to keep a racial equality perspective in all that they do. Educators need to be able to acquire information from a range of sources. A small but relevant library of books, tapes, videos and important journal articles on both theory and practice, is a vital resource, supporting and supplementing the staff development sessions.

A staff library will stimulate reading and reflection on particular aspects of anti-racist understandings and practices and the sharing of knowledge. One educator who has a particular interest in music, art, technology, outdoor play, children's self-esteem or working with parents, could research that topic for others. Educators will inevitably have different strengths, enthusiasms and interests and everyone should be willing to share the learning without competing. As with any academic study, criticism must be constructive, and understood as such always.

We must remember that we all learn in very different ways and that we all need encouragement and support to learn. A loan library can help people to learn at their own pace outside of staff development sessions. Different texts can alert staff to the fact that authors hold different perspectives. The loan library should be organised in a way that is accessible to all educators. Staff will have to decide whether parents should be allowed to borrow from the collection.

Information services are available to the setting that are well worth using, for instance, nurseries and schools can use the schools library service. The local authority may have a multicultural or multilingual support service that lends resources. It is also worth subscribing to the most relevant journals and buying books which have been carefully selected. Staff should also utilise their professional associations and unions, who might have published material which can be helpful to early years work. It is also worth finding out what is available from the various early years organisations by writing to the PPA, NNEB, NCMA, NCB and the Schools Curriculum and Assessment Authority (SCAA) (addresses at end of chapter).

With staff constantly learning more about equality issues, the philosophy of the early years setting will come under constant review to provide the best possible service.

5. Look at what is positive and what needs further attention in your existing curriculum.

Educators should not assume that everything about their practice will need changing. It is hopeful and positive to begin with the areas of the curriculum where staff feel they are best achieving a high standard which takes account of racial equality.

Traditionally, some areas of the curriculum have been seen as more applicable to racial equality than others. For instance, there may be a variety of different foods being cooked with the children, or a range of language activities which support bilingualism. Language, cookery, art and dressing-up clothes are some of the areas where multicultural and racial equality activities emerge, and these are all good starting points. Areas of the curriculum (hidden and overt) which rarely deal with racial equality tend to relate to science, numeracy, dealing with name-calling or parental support. Yet there are just as many opportunities here, and indeed they might be even more significantly helpful.

Identifying where the gaps are will help to ascertain where to go next. It may seem like a long way for some settings but it is important to take things slowly. Educators might, for instance, want to begin by reviewing the food experiences children have in their setting or the positive self-image work they undertake with children.

If the staff have a strong, developed sense of trust and a tradition of collaborative support it is worth trying to locate the setting within the perspectives identified in the earlier chapter on curriculum. It is likely that there will be an overlap between the perspectives we outlined — separatist, assimilationist, multiculturalist and anti-racist. This is not to suggest the setting should be put in a pigeon hole. The activity would raise discussion about curriculum and perhaps about what position the setting should be taking. The perspectives outlined are crude and should only be used as indicators to stimulate discussion.

6. Arrange workshops to identify racism in children's resources and to try out anti-racist resources

Early years educators need to try out and discuss the resources they acquire for promoting racial equality curricula for the children. This helps raise the kinds of issues which children themselves might face or raise. When educators use the resources for the first time the same questions usually arise! So the exercise helps both to prepare our answers and to evaluate the appropriateness of the resource.

Existing resources should also be scrutinised for racist messages. One good strategy is to hold a workshop on children's books, where a selection of information, reading/story books and possibly comics is analysed for racial stereotypes. There are many guides which can help educators to identify racist bias. The Working Group Against Racism in Children's Resources (WGARCR) has produced guidelines for the evaluation and selection of toys and other resources for children. This is a useful tool to have available at workshops (address for WGARCR at end of this chapter).

WGARCR chart the resources which could be explored in any early years setting, such as dolls, toys that aid literacy and numeracy development, home corner, jigsaws, puzzles and musical instruments. Workshops which highlight the presence of racist resources or the absence of anti-racist ones can be used positively. Educators can write to publishers and toy manufacturers to emphasise the need and demand for good quality antiracist materials.

7. Using outsiders and attending conferences

Educators may well find that their own expertise and skills are not enough for some specialist issues, and that the literature on some subjects is not sufficiently practical or helpful. Speakers from outside the setting can be invited to come and introduce or give practical support on a particular topic. For instance, the relevance or importance of bilingual education may be difficult for some educators to understand; others might feel that they need more practical advice about it from a specialist. Even if a setting has bilingual staff it cannot be assumed that they automatically know how to provide the right support — after all they probably followed the same courses as other colleagues.

Sometimes calling in an outside speaker or workshop leader just provides a fresh perspective on a particular issue. If possible, share what you are trying to achieve with ethnic minority and black members of the community. They may be able to offer support or advice and would certainly be interested and reassured that the educators take racial equality seriously. Speakers should not be exploited and, especially if they are members of the local community, their time and effort should be fully recognised and when appropriate rewarded. In time, as the confidence of all staff grows, the parents should be informed of the changes being implemented and asked for their advice, help and support in realising the set goals.

Most early years organisations hold regular conferences, locally and nationally. Some of these focus on issues of racial equality. Educators should try to attend such courses. Indeed, given the paucity of time allocated to equality issues on most initial training courses, conferences dealing specifically with racial equality should be made a priority.

8. Learning about the cultures, languages and history of black and ethnic minority groups in Britain

This book has attempted to give some information and guidance in this area, but is no substitute for wider reading and discussion with ethnic minority and black community members. Those educators who have had little contact with ethnic minorities and their languages, culture or history will find it very difficult to provide a balanced education incorporating racial equality issues. As suggested here, learning from up-to-date sources and then sharing this with colleagues provides a very positive way forward.

9. Monitoring and evaluating the change process

We cannot go through a series of in-service training sessions on any topic and then tick it off as done. Training is just the beginning. Just as staff development in the area of parental partnership or children's psycho-social development are on-going concerns for educators — and so should the issue of racial equality be. The many sessions of talking, re-writing policies or attending conferences and workshops would be a waste of time unless practice is carefully monitored.

New ideas do not penetrate practice immediately. Confidence in using the newly gained knowledge, skills, attitudes and concepts will take time. These new ideas can be lost if they are not re-introduced at regular meetings. Racial equality issues should permeate all aspects of practice. A discussion by educators on the changing of displays in the foyer of a setting, for example, if related to a common theme such as Harvest, could end up as completely ethnocentric. However, if educators have accommodated a racial equality perspective, the display would be sure to represent a variety of different cultural products, most of which would be familiar to all of the children.

The new knowledge must also inform the way children are assessed and individual records kept. Sensitive educators would make sure that records included information on the child's whole linguistic background and not just their competence in English, and that regular observations of children take this aspect of their development into account. Similarly we may need to monitor other policies and changes such as those concerned with the food served in the setting or the staff procedures for dealing with racist incidents. It is á good idea to put on record some of the changes that are to be made and then to evaluate them to see how much progress has been made, and/or to thrash out any problems.

The process by which change occurs — an example

Figure 8.4 shows the areas that were considered by one infant school staff in setting up their staff development programme. Most of the time was spent on consciousness raising, attitudes and policy, and it took a year of fortnightly meetings to work through all the issues. The in-service provision allowed flexibility as the programme developed and an anti-racist context was being created. Along the way, the group leader monitored the progress achieved, in consultation with the teachers. She set up a structure for evaluating the quality of practice. It was obvious that at the end of the year there were varying levels of commitment from staff, but most had achieved a good grasp of the main concepts and had changed some of their attitudes and practice. It was only after this lengthy process that the staff felt confident enough to approach parents for support, and to support them in their understandings. Staff claimed that this in-service programme had been invaluable in helping their confidence, and that the newly acquired knowledge assisted them in offering a better service to both parents and children.

Working together for change

In an in-service programme of this nature educators need first to establish ground rules. Sensitive issues will inevitably be the focus of some discussions and educators might have their long- held beliefs challenged. This will not be easy for the individuals concerned nor, sometimes, for the group. Educators should work on this first before embarking on a series of meetings. Some of the following ground rules may act as a guide, but are not meant to be prescriptive:

☐ everyone should have the right to be listened to and any misgivings they hold should be aired openly;

☐ any expressions of anger or hostility should be dealt with constructively and without judgement upon the person/s uttering them;

THE CHANGE PROCESS
what happened in one school

1. **Changing our own consciousness and attitudes**

   a) specialist training

   b) learning from others: LEAs/unions, schools, voluntary groups/advisers/community organisations (Black & White)

2. **Changing the school policy**

   a) Hidden curriculum

   — organisation of resources

   — creating an anti-racist ethos

   — independent work/group work

   — parents, governors

   b) Curriculum

   — developing areas most suitable for anti-racist education

   — teaching and learning through a thematic approach

   — language awareness and bilingual support

   — anti-racism across the curriculum, tackling areas like science and maths

   — curriculum innovations by specialists

3. **In-service provision**

   — using LEA/voluntary agencies

   — role of the headteacher/group leader

   — how to create an anti-racist ethos

   — use of journals and relevant organisations.

☐ it must be recognised that everyone will be starting from different positions, with different understandings and biases;

☐ it should be acknowledged that some people may experience hurt and pain during the process of facing challenging new ideas;

☐ everyone should agree to treat the meetings as confidential to the staff concerned;

☐ everyone should trust others to work towards change and should come to conclusions together;

☐ each person should choose a 'critical friend(s)' to share their ideas and practice with on a day-to-day basis; and

☐ it should be recognised that not *all* our attempts at understanding new ideas or trying out new practices will work first time round.

Useful Sources and Resources for Racial Equality

Afro-Caribbean Resource Centre (ACER)*
Wyvil School, Wyvil Road, London, SW8 2TJ. Tel. 0181-627 2662

Access to Information on Multicultural Education Resources (AIMER)
Reading and Language Centre, University of Reading, Bulmershe Court, Reading, RG6 lHY. Tel. (01734) 875123 Extn. 4871

Childsplay (Toyshop)
112, Tooting High Street, London, SW17 ORR

Commission for Racial Equality
Elliot House, 10-12, Allington Street, London, SWlE 5EH.
Tel. 0171-828 7022

Council for Inter-racial Books for Children*
1841, Broadway, New York, NY 10023, U.S.A.

Council of Europe
(School Education Division) 67006 Strasbourg Cedex, France.

Development Education Centre*
(for anti-racism training resources and packs)
998, Bristol Road, Selly Oak, Birmingham, B29 6LE. Tel. 0121- 472 3255

Early Years Trainers Anti-Racist Network (EYTARN)
1, The Lyndens, 51, Granville Road, London, N12 OJH

Education and Equality (in Women's Employment)
23, Merton Road, Mosely, Birmingham, B13 9BX

Equality Learning Centre
Save the Children and London Voluntary Sector Resource Centre
356 Holloway Road, London N7 6PA. Tel: 0171-700 8127

Equal Opportunities Commission
Overseas House, Quay Street, Manchester, M3 3HN. Tel. 0161-833 9244

Free Kindergarten Association*
(FKA) (posters, information, books on bilingualism, videos)
Multicultural Resource Centre, 1st Floor, 9-11, Stewart Street, Richmond,
3121 Victoria, Australia

Intermediate Technology
(cross-cultural technology, packs, slides and posters)
Myson House, Railway Terrace, Rugby, CV21 3HT. Tel. (01788) 560631

Letterbox Library*
(for children's books)
Unit 2D, Leroy House, 436, Essex Road, London, Nl 3QP. Tel.0171-226 1633

Local Community Relations Councils and Multi-Cultural Education Resource Centres
Contact through local telephone directory.

Magi Publications
(books)
55, Crowland Avenue, Hayes, Middx.

Mantra Publications
5, Alexandra Grove, London, N12 8NU

Minority Rights Group
Education department 379, Brixton Road, London, SW9 7DE
Tel.0171-978 9498

National Association for the Teaching of English
50, Broadfield Road, Broadfield Business Centre, Sheffield, S8 OXJ
Tel. (01742) 555419

National Childminding Association*
8 Masons Hill, Bromley, Kent, BR2 9EY. Tel. 0181-464 6164

Council for Awards in Childcare and Education (previously NNEB)*
8, Chequer Street, St. Albans, Herts. ALl 3XZ. Tel. (01727) 867333

National Religious Education Centre
West London Institute, Lancaster House, Borough Road, Isleworth, Middx.
TW7 5DU. Tel. 0181-568 8741

National Children's Bureau*
Early Childhood Unit, 8, Wakley Street, London EClV 7QE
Tel.0171-278 9441

Pre-School Playgroups Association (PPA)*
PPA National Centre, 61-63, Kings Cross Road, London WClX 9LL
Tel.0171-833 0991

The Runnymede Trust*
11, Princelet Street, London, El 6QH. Tel.0171-375 1496

Save the Children
Education Unit, Save the Children,17, Grove End, London SE5 8RD
Tel. 0171-703 5400

Soma Books
38, Kennington Lane, London, SEll 4LS. Tel. 0171-735 2101

Tamarind*
(for children's books and puzzles)
Child's Play (International) Ltd., Ashworth Road, Bridgemead, Swindon, SN5 7YD. Tel. (01793) 616286

Trentham Books
Westview House, 734, London Road, Stoke-on-Trent, ST4 5NP.
Tel. (01782) 745567

The Citizenship Foundation
63, Charterhouse Street" London, EClM 6HJ. Tel.0171-253 4480

Voluntary Organisations Liaison
Council for Under-Fives (VOLCUF)
77, Holloway Road, London, N7 8JZ

Working Group Against Racism in Children's Resources (WGRCR)*
460, Wandsworth Road, London, SW8 3LX

* *especially recommended*

Bibliography

Alexander, R., Rose, J., Woodhead, C., (1992) *Curriculum Organisation and Classroom Practice in Practice in Primary Schools*, HMSO.

Atkinson, D. (ed) (1989) *The Children's Bookroom*, Trentham.

Bakar, Denham, Meikle and Rano (1991) *Playing in Harmony, An Early Years Resource Pack*, Save the Children (Scotland).

Barrett, G. (1986) *Starting School: an Evaluation of the Experience*, Association of Masters and Mistresses.

Barrett, G. (ed) *Disaffection from School? The Early Years*, Falmer Press.

Bernstein, B. (1970) 'Education Cannot Compensate for Society' in *New Society*, 26.2.70, pp.344-7.

Biggs, A.P., Edwards, A.V., (1992) 'I treat them all the same' 'Teacher-Pupil Talk in Multi-ethnic Classrooms' in *Language and Education*, Vol.5, No.3, pp.161-176.

Birch, B. (1985) *A Question of Race*, MacDonald.

Brennan, J. McGeevor, P. (1987) *Employment of Graduates from Ethnic Minorities*, Commission for Racial Equality.

Bruce, T. (1987) *Early Childhood Education*, Hodder and Stoughton.

Bryant, P. (1974) *Perception and Understanding in Young Children*, Methuen.

Burns, R. (1982) *Self-Concept, Development and Education*, Holt, Rinehart and Winston.

Carter, T. (1986) *Shattering Illusions: West Indians in British Politics*, Lawrence and Wishart.

Cashmore and Troyna (1990) *Introduction to Race Relations*, Falmer Press 2nd Edition.

Clarke, P. and Millikan, J. (1986) *Developing Multicultural Perspectives in Early Childhood*, Free Kindergarten Association, Multicultural Resource Centre.

Clarke, P. (1992) *English as a 2nd Language in Early Childhood*, Multicultural Resource Centre: Australia.

Cohn, T. (1987) 'Sticks and Stones may break my bones but names will never hurt me' in *Multicultural Teaching*, Vol.5, No.3.

Commission for Racial Equality, (1986) *Formal Investigation into Calderdale LEA*, E2L provision, CRE.

Commission for Racial Equality, (1986) *Teaching English as a Second Language*, CRE.

Commission for Racial Equality, (1989) *Code of Practice: For the Elimination of Racial Discrimination in Education*, CRE.

Commission for Racial Equality, (1989) *From Cradle to School*, Commission for Racial Equality.

Conteh, J. (1992) 'Monolingual children and language diversity: the space in the centre' *Multicultural Teaching*, Vol.11, pp.1-5.

Cowley, L. (ed) (1991) *Young Children in Group Day Care — Guidelines for Good Practice*, National Children's Bureau.

Craft, M. and Craft, A. (1981) *The Participation of Ethnic Minorities in Further and Higher Education*, Oxford, Nuffield Foundation.

Cross, W.E. (1985) 'Black Identity: Rediscovering the distinctions personal identity and reference group orientation' In Spencer, M.B. et al (eds.) *Beginnings: the Social and Affective Development of Black Children*, (pp.155-172) Hillsdale, N.J. Erlbaum.

Cummins, J. (1984) Bilingualism and Special Education: Issues in Assessment and Pedagogy, *Multilingual Matters 6*.

Curtis, A. (1991) *Early Childhood Education Explained*, OMEP (UK) Publications.

Davey, A. (1983) *Learning to be Prejudiced: Growing up in Multiethnic Britain*, Edward Arnold.

Dermon-Sparks, L. (1989) *Anti-Bias Curriculum*, National Association for the Education of Young Children. Washington D.C.

Department of Education and Science (1985) *Education for All*, The Swann Report, HMSO.

Department of Education and Science (1989) *The Education of Children Under Five*, HMSO.

Department of Education and Science (1990) *Starting with Quality*, HMSO.

Development Education Centre (1990) *What is a Family?* Development Education Centre, Birmingham.

Donaldson, M. (1978) *Children's Minds*, Fontana.

Donaldson, M. (1992) *Human Minds*, Penguin Press.

Donoghue, J. (1991) Entitlement for All: Race, Gender and ERA—A Perspective from the NCC in *Multicultural Teaching*, Vol.10, No.1.

Drummond, M.J., Lally, M. and Pugh, G. (1989) *Developing a Curriculum for the Early Years*, National Children's Bureau.

Drummond, M.J. and Rouse, D. and Pugh, G. (eds) (1992) *Making Assessment Work*, National Children's Bureau.

Early Childhood Unit (1991) *Ensuring Standards in the Care of Young Children, Registering and Developing Quality Day Care*, National Children's Bureau.

Early Years Curriculum Group (1989) *The Early Years Curriculum and the National Curriculum*, Trentham Books.

Early Years Curriculum Group (1992) *First Things First: Educating Young Children*, Madeleine Lindley Ltd: Oldham.

Edwards, V. (1983) *Education in Multicultural Classrooms*, Batsford Academic.

Epstein, D., and Sealey, A. (1990) *Where It Really Matters': Developing anti-racist education in predominantly white primary schools*, Development Education Centre, Birmingham.

Early Year's Trainers Anti-Racist Network (1991) Early Years Anti-Racist Practice, Legislation and Research, A Conference Report.

Fitzpatrick, F. (1987) *The Open Door*, Multilingual Matters.

Flynn, R. and Phoenix, A. (1988) *Racism and the Child Care Services* OMEP (UK) Update No.25.

Gay, G. (1985) 'Implications of Selected Models of Ethnic Identity Development for Educators' in the *Journal of Negro Education*, Vol.54, No.1.

Gilkes, J. (1987) *Developing Nursery Education*, Open University Press.

Gilroy, P. (1987) *There Ain't No Black In the Union Jack*, Hutchinson.

Gordon, P. and Newnham, A. (1986) *Different Worlds: Racism and Discrimination in Britain*, Runnymede Trust.

Gordon, P. (1990) *Racial Violence and Harassment,* Runnymede Trust.

Hall, J., Porter, C., Clarke, (1989) *Incorporating a Multicultural Perspective Programme: Planning for Early Childhood*, Free Kindergarten Assoc. Multicultural Resource Centre: Australia.

Hazareesingh, S., Simms, K., Anderson, P. (1989) *Educating the Whole Child,* Save the Children.

Her Majesty's Stationary Office (1988) *Education Reform Act.* HMSO

Her Majesty's Stationary Office (1989) *Children Act.* HMSO

Home Office Report (1983) *Ethnic Minorities in Britain.* HMSO.

Hurst, V. (1991) *Planning for Early Learning and Education in the First Five Years*, Paul Chapman Pubs. Ltd.

Inner London Education Authority (1986) *Nursery Rhyme or Reason*, ILEA.

Jones, Crispin (1986) Racism in Society and Schools in Gundara, J. et al (eds) *Race, Diversity and Education*, Hodder.

Kelly, E. and Cohn, T. (1988) *Racism in Schools — New Research Evidence*, Trentham Books.

Klein, G. (1993) *Education Towards Race Equality*, Cassell.

Kutner, B. (1955) Patterns of mental functioning associated with 'prejudice in children' in *Psychological Monographs* 72(406), pp.1-48.

Lally, M. (1991) *The Nursery Teacher in Action*, Paul Chapman.

Lane, J. (1990) 'Sticks and Carrots' *Local Government Policy Making,* Vol.17, No.3.

Lawrence, D. (1988) *Enhancing self-esteem in the classroom*, Paul Chapman.

Lothian Regional Council (1992) *Lothian Children's Family Charter*, LRC

Maximé, J.E. (1991) 'Towards a Transcultural Approach to Working with Under-Sevens' in the Report of Two Conferences Combating Racism Among Students, Staff and Children, Nursery Nurse Trainers. Early Years Anti Racist Network and National Children's Bureau.

McIntosh, N. Smith, D. (1976) *The Extent of Racial Disadvantage*, PEP, Vol. 40, No.547.

Miles, R. (1982) *Racism and Migrant Labour,* Routledge and Kegan Paul

Milner, D. (1983) *Children and Race: 10 years on*, Ward Lock Educational

Moyles, J. (1989) *Just Playing? The Role and Status of Play in Early Childhood Education*, Open University Press.

Murphy, L. (1989) The Combined Nursery Centre National Association of Nursery Centres, Open University B.Phil. Dissertation.

Murphy, P. (1989) 'Assessment and gender' in *NUT Education Review*, Equal Opportunities in the New ERA, Vol.3, No.2.

Myers, R. (1992) *The Twelve Who Survive*, Routledge.

National Curriculum Council (1991) A Pluralist Society in the Classroom and Beyond, *NCC Newsletter,* No.5.

National Curriculum Council (1992) *Starting Out with the National Curriculum*, NCC.

National Union of Teachers (1989) 'Equal Opportunities and the ERAS *NUT Education Review*.

Newell, P. (1991) *The United National Convention and Children's Rights in the U.K.* National Children's Bureau, London.

National Nursery Examination Board (1991) *The Diploma and Preliminary Diploma in Nursery Nursing*, (Draft) NNEB.

Nursery Nurse Trainers Anti-Racist Network (1987) *Selecting Students: to ensure equality of opportunity*, (NNTARN)

Ogilvy, Booth, Cheyne, Jahoda and Schaffer (1990) 'Staff attitudes and perception in multicultural nursery schools' *Early Child Development and Care*, Vol.64.

Pinsent, P. (ed) (1992) *Language, Culture and Young Children*, Fulton.

Policy Studies Institute Report (1984) *Black and White Britain*, PSI.

Pre-school Playgroups Association (1989a) *Guidelines: Good Practice for Full Daycare Playgroups*, PPA.

Pre-school Playgroups Association (1989b) *Guidelines: Good Practice for Sessional Playgroups*, PPA.

Pre-school Playgroups Association (1991a) *Information Sheet 5 'Equal Opportunities Policy Statements*, PPA.

Pre-school Playgroups Association (1991b) *Equal Chances*, PPA.

Pre-school Playgroups Association (1992) *Early Care and Education — What Playgroups Need in the 1990s*, Report PPA.

Pugh, G. and De'Ath, E. (1984) *The Needs of Parents: Practice and Policy in Parent Education*, Macmillan.

Pugh, G. and De'Ath, E. (1989) *Working Towards Partnership in the Early Years*, National Children's Bureau.

Pugh, G. (1992) *Contemporary Issues in the Early Years*, Paul Chapman.

Pugh, et al (1987) *Partnership in Action: Working with parents in pre-school centres*, National Children's Bureau.

Purkey, W. (1970) *Self-Concept and School Achievement*, London, Paul Chapman.

Rattansi, A. and Donald, J. (1992) *Course Introduction: The Question of Racism*, The Open University.

Reeves, F. and Chevannes, M. (1981) 'The Underachievement of Rampton' *Multicultural Education*, Vol.10, No.1, pp.35-42.

Richardson, R. (1990) *Daring to be a Teacher*, Trentham Books.

Ross, C. and Ryan, A. (1990) *'Can I Stay In Today Miss?' Improving the School Playground*, Trentham Books.

Rouse, D., Griffin, S. (1992) 'Quality for the Under Three's' in Pugh, G. (ed) *Contemporary Issues in the Early Years*, PCP, pp.138-156.

Rowling, N. (1987) *Commodities: How the World was taken to Market*, Free Association Books for Channel Four.

Runnymede Trust (1993) Equality Assurance in Schools:, Trentham Books.

Siraj-Blatchford, I. (1990) 'Access to what? Black students' perceptions of initial teacher education' *Journal of Access Studies*, Vol.5, No.2, Aut. 1990.

Siraj-Blatchford, I. (1990) 'A Positive Role', *Child Education*, November 1990.

Siraj-Blatchford, I. (1992) 'Why Understanding Cultural Differences is Not Enough' in Pugh, G. (ed) 1992 op. cit. pp104- 121.

Stone, M. (1981) *The Education of the Black Child in Britain: The Myth of Multiracial Education*, Fontana.

Stonehouse, A. (1991) *Opening the Doors: Childcare in a Multicultural Society*, Australian Early Childhood Assoc. Inc.

Sylva, K., Siraj-Blatchford, I., Johnson, S., (1992). 'The Impact of the U.K. National Curriculum on Pre-school Practice' in *International Journal of Early Childhood*, Vol.24, No.1, pp.41-51.

Sylva, K. Lunt, I. (1982) *Child Development: A First Course*, Basil Blackwell.

Sylva, K., Roy, C. and Painter, M. (1980) *Childwatching at Playgroup and Nursery School*, Grant McIntyre.

Sylva, K., Campbell, R.J., Coates, E., David, T., Fitzgerald, J., Goodyear, R., Jowett, M., Lewis, A. and Neill, S. St.J. (1990) *Assessing Three to Eight Year Olds*, National Foundation for Educational Research.

Timyan, J. (1988) 'Cultural Aspects of Psycho-social Development: An Examination of West African Childrearing Practices'. Report for UNICEF Conference January 1988, New York.

Tomlinson, S. (1990) *Multicultural Education in all White Schools*. Batsford.

Tomlinson, S. (1980) 'The Educational Performance of Ethnic Minority Children' in *New Community*, Vol.18, No.3. pp.213-34.

Troyna, B. and Hatcher, R. (1992) *Racism in Children's lives*, Routledge and National Children's Bureau.

Troyna and Hatcher (1992) 'Racist incidents in schools: a framework for analysis' in Gill, Mayor and Blair (Eds.) *Racism and Education*, Sage.

Twitchin, J. and Demuth, C. (1985) *Multicultural Education*, BBC Publications.

Under Fives Unit (1990) *A Policy for Young Children: A framework for Action*, National Children's Bureau.

Verhallen, M., Appel, R., Schoonen, R., (1989) 'Language Functions in Early Childhood Education: the Cognitive — Linquistic Experiences of Bilingual and Monolingual Children' in *Language and Education*, Vol.3, No.2, pp.109-130.

Vygotsky, L.S. (1986, 3rd Ed.) *Thought and Language*, Cambridge, Mass, The M.I.T. Press.

Working Group Against Racism In Children's Resources (1990) *Guidelines for the Evaluation and Selection of Toys and other Resources for Children,* WCARCR.

Wright, C. (1992) 'Early Education: Multiracial Primary School Classrooms' in Gill, D. et al *Racism and Education*, Sage.

Wright, J. (1977) *Bilingualism in Education*, CUES Occ. Paper No.1.

Yeatman, A. (1988) *A review of multicultural policies and programs in children's services*. Canberra: Office of Multicultural Affairs: Australia.

Index

Abuse 66
access 131
America 46
ancillary staff 155
anti-bias 150
anti-racist 69
assessment 36, 41, 48, 88, 90, 144
assimilation 68
assumptions 45
Australia 48

Babies 34, 36
behaviour 85
books 42, 76
    favourite 59
    selection 78

Canada 46
child-centred 51, 64, 66
childhood 26, 64
childrearing 64, 72, 96, 102-104
Children Act 93, 129, 133-139
communication 36, 56, 115
community 33
Creoles 52
cultural 28
    analysis 43
    heritage 42
    superiority 62
    values 26, 30

curriculum 67
    cross curricular themes 71
    definition 62
Democracy 34
discrimination 132

Early Years Curriculum Group 63
Early Years Trainers Anti-Racist
    Network 115, 118
Education Reform Act, 70, 91, 129,
    139
empathy 40
empire 14-15
employment 17
ethnic cleansing 62
ethno-centrism 104, 135
Europe 13-14, 44, 46

Families 51, 70, 92, 98, 130, 149
first language 54
flannel board 42, 59
food 82, 84

Governors 148
group work 74

Hillfields Nursery Centre 110

ILEA 117
images 25, 101
injustice 62

institutional racism 16, 21, 130

Literature 29, 43
listening 36
linguistic racism 47
language awareness 60, 79
learning 76
LMS 140, 146
league tables 147

Management 128
media 23
mother-tongue 54
multiculturalist 68, 150
   resources 81
music 84

Name-calling 9, 11, 14, 87
National Curriculum Council 56,
   141-144, 71-141
National Vocational Qualification
   116-117, 124
Netherlands 44
non-verbal 86

Parents 52, 87, 90 93, 100
   and bilingualism 50
   charter 148
   education 94
   ethnic minority 51, 92, 103-105
   partnership 95
   responsibility 133
   rights 91
Physical characteristics 4
play 28, 38, 41, 73
policy statements 110-128, 157
   monitoring 127
profiles 49, 88
puppets 42, 59

Racial hierarchy 5
   harassment 10, 12, 87
   underachievement 8-9, 19
Race Relations Act 129-132, 136, 147
Records 49, 162
registration 134, 136
reviews 134
rhymes 35-36, 84

Scandinavia 46
segregation 130
selection criteria 78, 80
self identity 4, 6-9, 20, 33, 87, 154
separatist 67
silent period 53
socialisation 4, 23
songs 35-36, 79, 84
speech 39
standard English 43
Stereotyping 20, 24, 28, 65, 72, 80, 154

Talk 42
television 23
tests 19
third world 25
thought 33
toddlers 35-36, 98
training 45
transliteration 56

Unemployment 17
United Nations 100

Victimisation 132
vocabulary 38-39

White superiority 15
   children 8
Working class 51
Working Group Against Racism in
   Children's Resources 79, 160

Yugoslavia 62